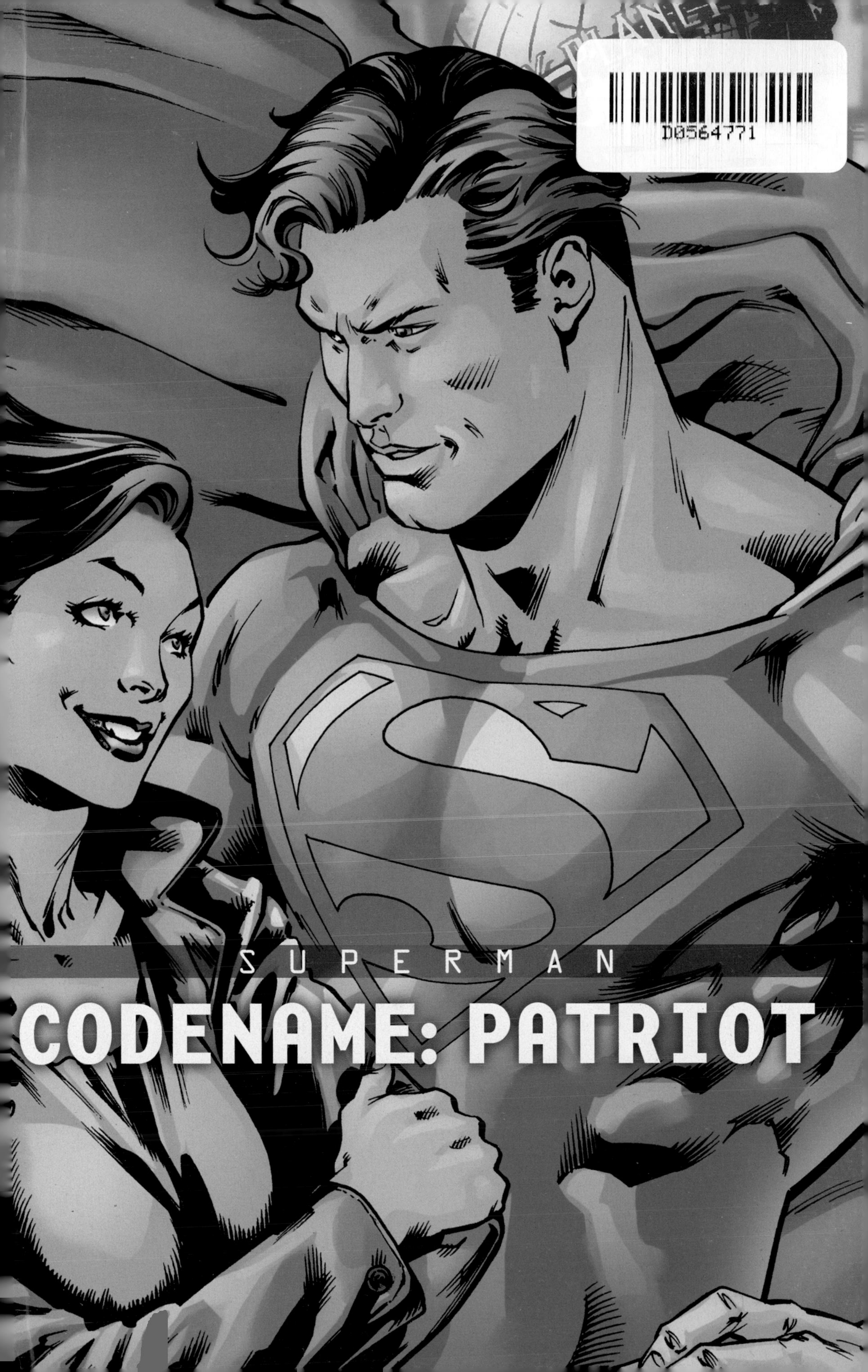
SUPERMAN
CODENAME: PATRIOT

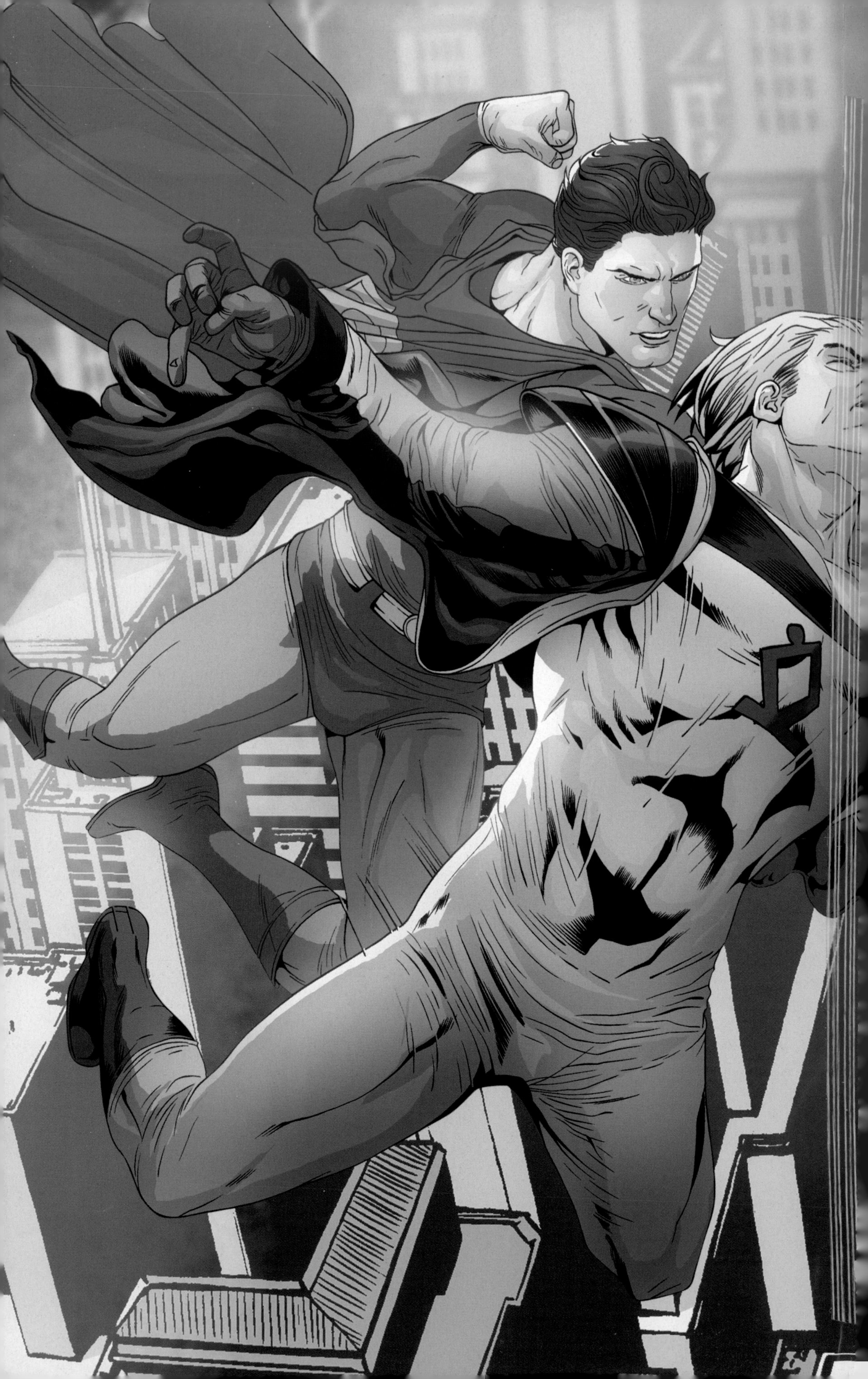

SUPERMAN
CODENAME: PATRIOT

**GREG RUCKA   JAMES ROBINSON
STERLING GATES**
<WRITERS>

**PETE WOODS   JULIÁN LÓPEZ
JAMAL IGLE   RENATO GUEDES
EDUARDO PANSICA   BERNARD CHANG**
<PENCILLERS>

**PETE WOODS   BIT
JON SIBAL   JOSÉ WILSON MAGALHÃES
SANDRO RIBEIRO   BERNARD CHANG**
<INKERS>

**BRAD ANDERSON   JAVIER MENA
NEI RUFFINO   DAVID CURIEL
MIKE THOMAS**
<COLORISTS>

**STEVE WANDS
ROB LEIGH   JARED K. FLETCHER
JOHN J. HILL   TRAVIS LANHAM**
<LETTERERS>

COVER ART BY **AARON LOPRESTI** WITH HI-FI
<SUPERMAN> CREATED BY JERRY SIEGEL AND JOE SHUSTER

DAN DIDIO <SVP-EXECUTIVE EDITOR> MATT IDELSON <EDITOR-ORIGINAL SERIES>
WIL MOSS <ASSISTANT EDITOR-ORIGINAL SERIES> GEORG BREWER <VP-DESIGN & DC DIRECT CREATIVE>
BOB HARRAS <GROUP EDITOR-COLLECTED EDITIONS> ANTON KAWASAKI <EDITOR>
ROBBIN BROSTERMAN <DESIGN DIRECTOR-BOOKS>

<DC COMICS>
PAUL LEVITZ <PRESIDENT & PUBLISHER> RICHARD BRUNING <SVP-CREATIVE DIRECTOR>
PATRICK CALDON <EVP-FINANCE & OPERATIONS> AMY GENKINS <SVP-BUSINESS & LEGAL AFFAIRS>
JIM LEE <EDITORIAL DIRECTOR-WILDSTORM> GREGORY NOVECK <SVP-CREATIVE AFFAIRS>
STEVE ROTTERDAM <SVP-SALES & MARKETING> CHERYL RUBIN <SVP-BRAND MANAGEMENT>

DC COMICS, 1700 BROADWAY, NEW YORK, NY 10019
A WARNER BROS. ENTERTAINMENT COMPANY
PRINTED BY RR DONNELLEY, SALEM, VA USA 3/11/11. FIRST PRINTING.
SC ISBN:978-1-4012-2657-2

SUSTAINABLE
FORESTRY
INITIATIVE

Certified Chain of Custody
Promoting Sustainable
Forest Management

Fiber used in this product line meets the
sourcing requirements of the SFI program.
www.sfiprogram.org NFS-SPICOC-C0001801

IT BEGAN WITH AN EPIC BATTLE

BETWEEN EARTH'S GREATEST HERO, SUPERMAN, AND THE EVIL ALIEN BRAINIAC. DURING THAT CLASH, SUPERMAN DISCOVERED THE LOST CITY OF KANDOR TRAPPED IN THE DEPTHS OF THE ALIEN'S SHIP, 100,000 KRYPTONIAN INHABITANTS INSIDE. SUPERMAN WAS REUNITED WITH HIS PEOPLE, BUT AT A HUGE PERSONAL COST: HE WAS UNABLE TO SAVE THE LIFE OF HIS ADOPTIVE FATHER, JONATHAN KENT.

KANDOR WAS FREED AND RELOCATED TO EARTH, BUT THE UNEASY ALLIANCE BETWEEN HUMANS AND KRYPTONIANS QUICKLY DEGENERATED INTO VIOLENCE AND TRAGEDY. A SECRET GOVERNMENT ORGANIZATION, PROJECT 7734, HELPED ORCHESTRATE THE AGGRESSION BETWEEN THE TWO RACES. 7734'S LEADER IS GENERAL SAM LANE, A MAN THOUGHT LONG DEAD, AND HE GAVE THE ORDER TO ASSASSINATE ZOR-EL, SUPERGIRL'S FATHER AND THE LEADER OF THE KRYPTONIANS. MEANWHILE, A TEAM OF KRYPTONIANS BRUTALLY MURDERED SEVERAL OF METROPOLIS'S SCIENCE POLICE ON AMERICAN SOIL.

IN AN EFFORT TO RESOLVE THE GROWING CONFLICT, ZOR-EL'S WIDOW, ALURA, TOOK CHARGE OF THE KRYPTONIANS AND COMBINED BRAINIAC'S TECHNOLOGY WITH KANDOR'S TO CREATE A NEW PLANET – NEW KRYPTON. THE PLANET ESTABLISHED AN ORBIT OPPOSITE EARTH'S OWN. IT APPEARED THAT THE CONFLICT HAD ENDED...BUT LOOKS CAN BE DECEIVING.

WHEN ALURA RELEASED GENERAL ZOD FROM THE PHANTOM ZONE AND GAVE HIM COMMAND OF NEW KRYPTON'S ARMY, SUPERMAN WAS FORCED TO MAKE THE HARDEST DECISION OF HIS LIFE: HE WOULD MOVE TO NEW KRYPTON TO KEEP ZOD IN CHECK.

AMID THE ESCALATING TENSIONS AND SUPERMAN'S ABSENCE, NEW AND OLD HEROES ALIKE HAVE RISEN TO PROTECT THE EARTH. NOW THEY MUST UNITE FOR THE FIRST TIME TO KEEP THE FRAGILE PEACE BETWEEN EARTH AND NEW KRYPTON...

<SUPERMAN: WORLD OF NEW KRYPTON 6>
COVER ART BY **FERNANDO DAGNINO** & **RAÚL FERNANDEZ** WITH **MAZI**

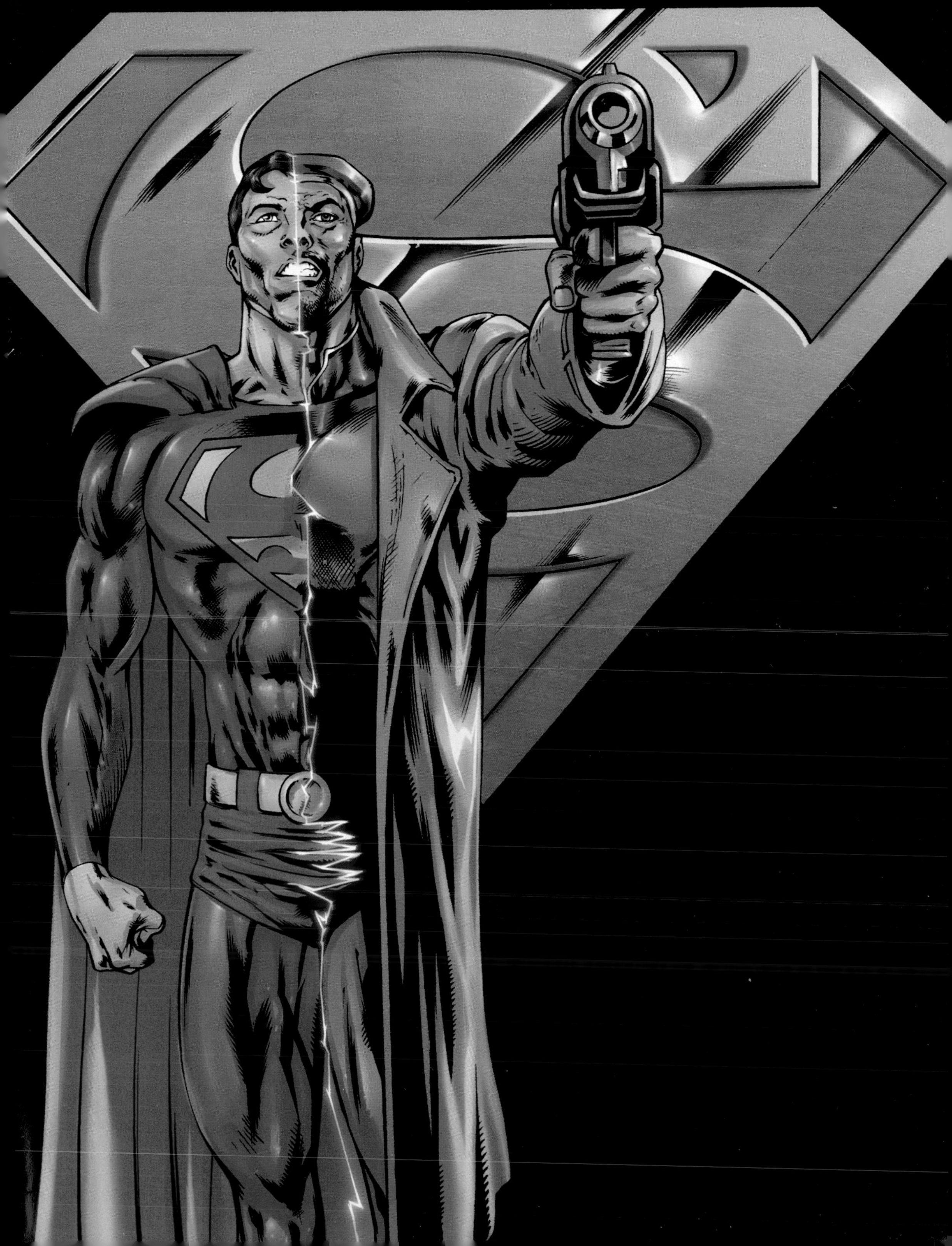

CODENAME: PATRIOT <PART ONE>

GREG RUCKA & JAMES ROBINSON – WRITERS
PETE WOODS – ARTIST

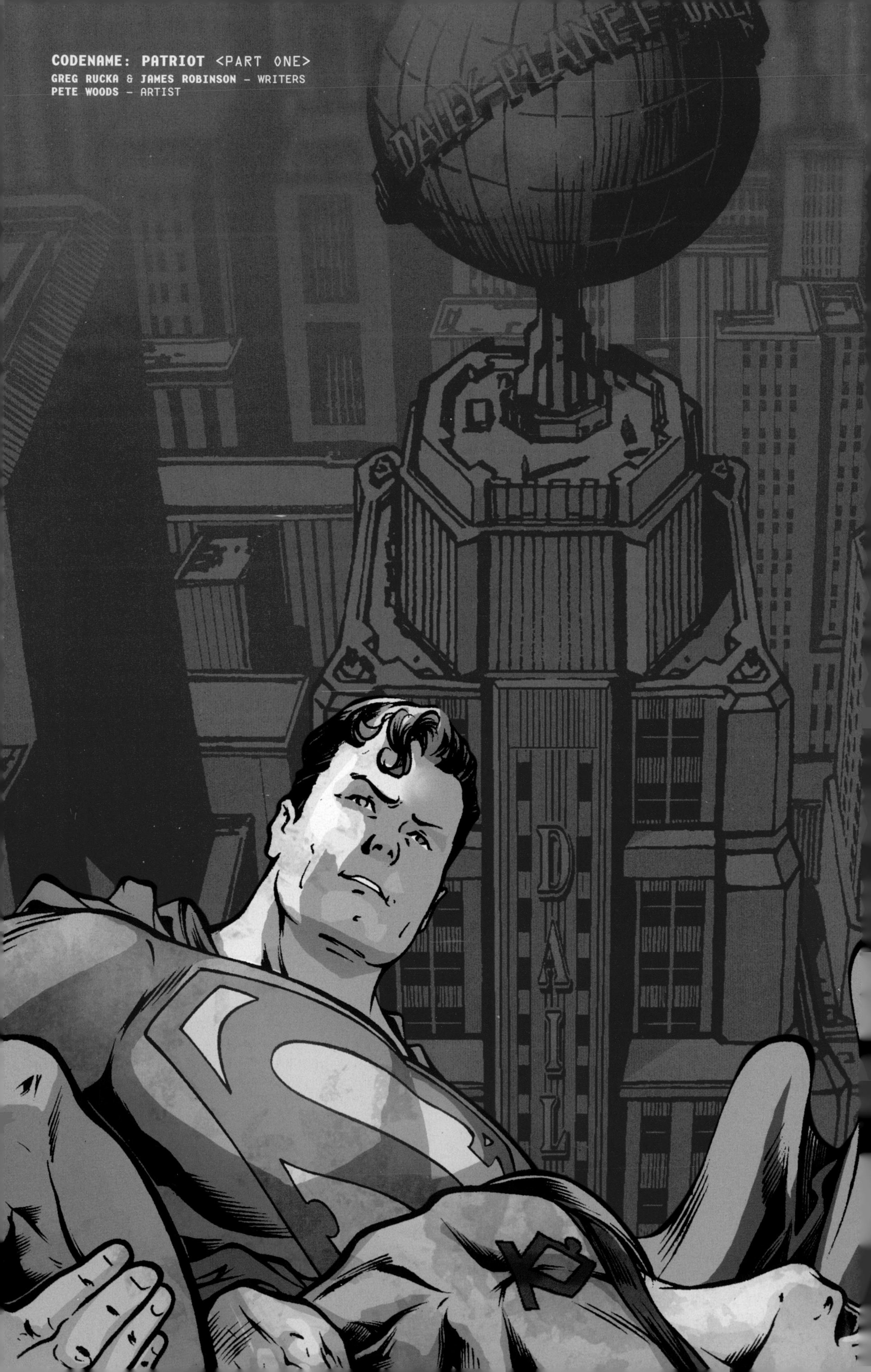
DAILY PLANET
DAILY

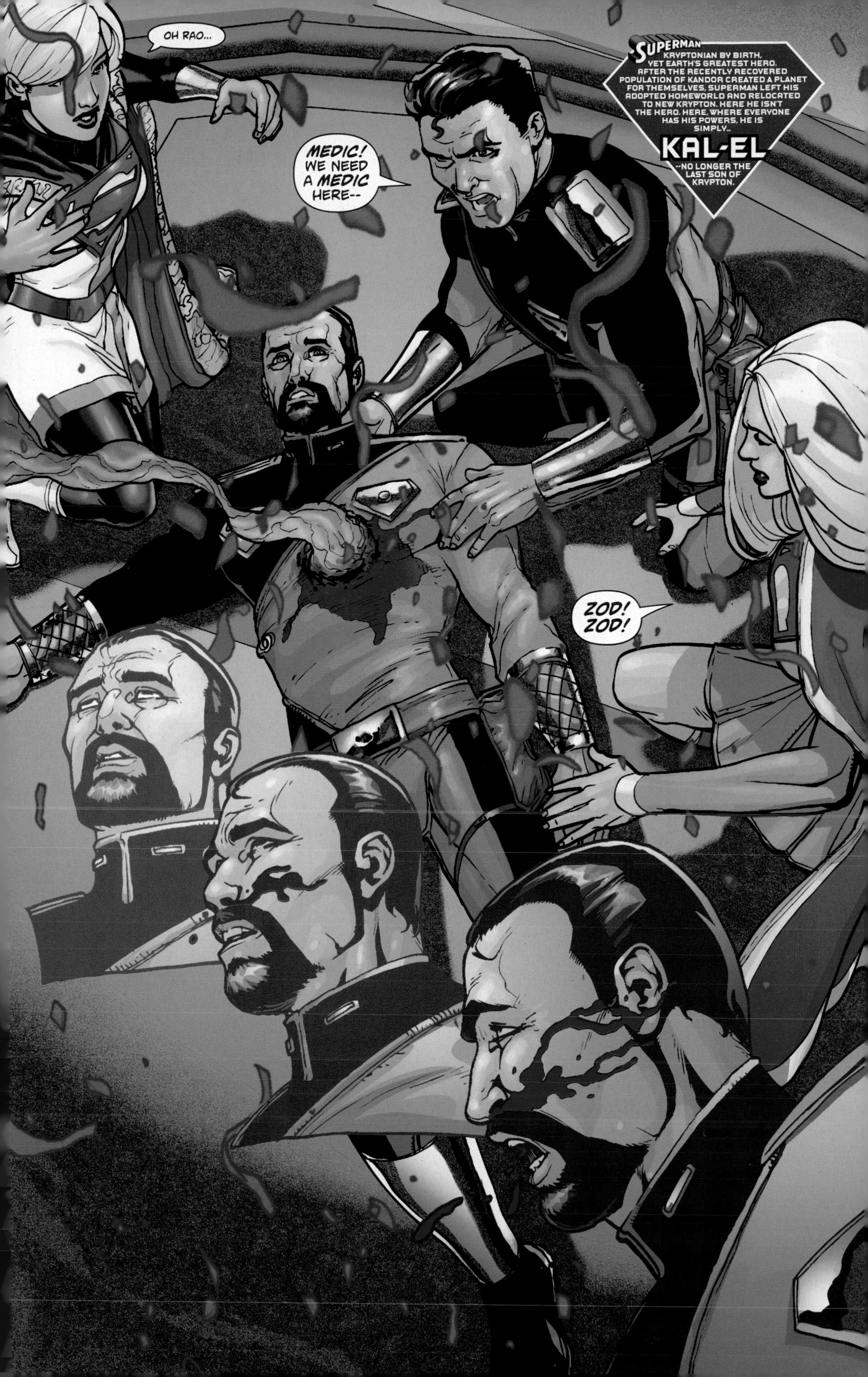
OH RAO...
SUPERMAN
KRYPTONIAN BY BIRTH, YET EARTH'S GREATEST HERO. AFTER THE RECENTLY RECOVERED POPULATION OF KANDOR CREATED A PLANET FOR THEMSELVES, SUPERMAN LEFT HIS ADOPTED HOMEWORLD AND RELOCATED TO NEW KRYPTON. HERE HE ISN'T THE HERO. HERE, WHERE EVERYONE HAS HIS POWERS, HE IS SIMPLY...
KAL-EL
--NO LONGER THE LAST SON OF KRYPTON.
MEDIC! WE NEED A MEDIC HERE--
ZOD! ZOD!

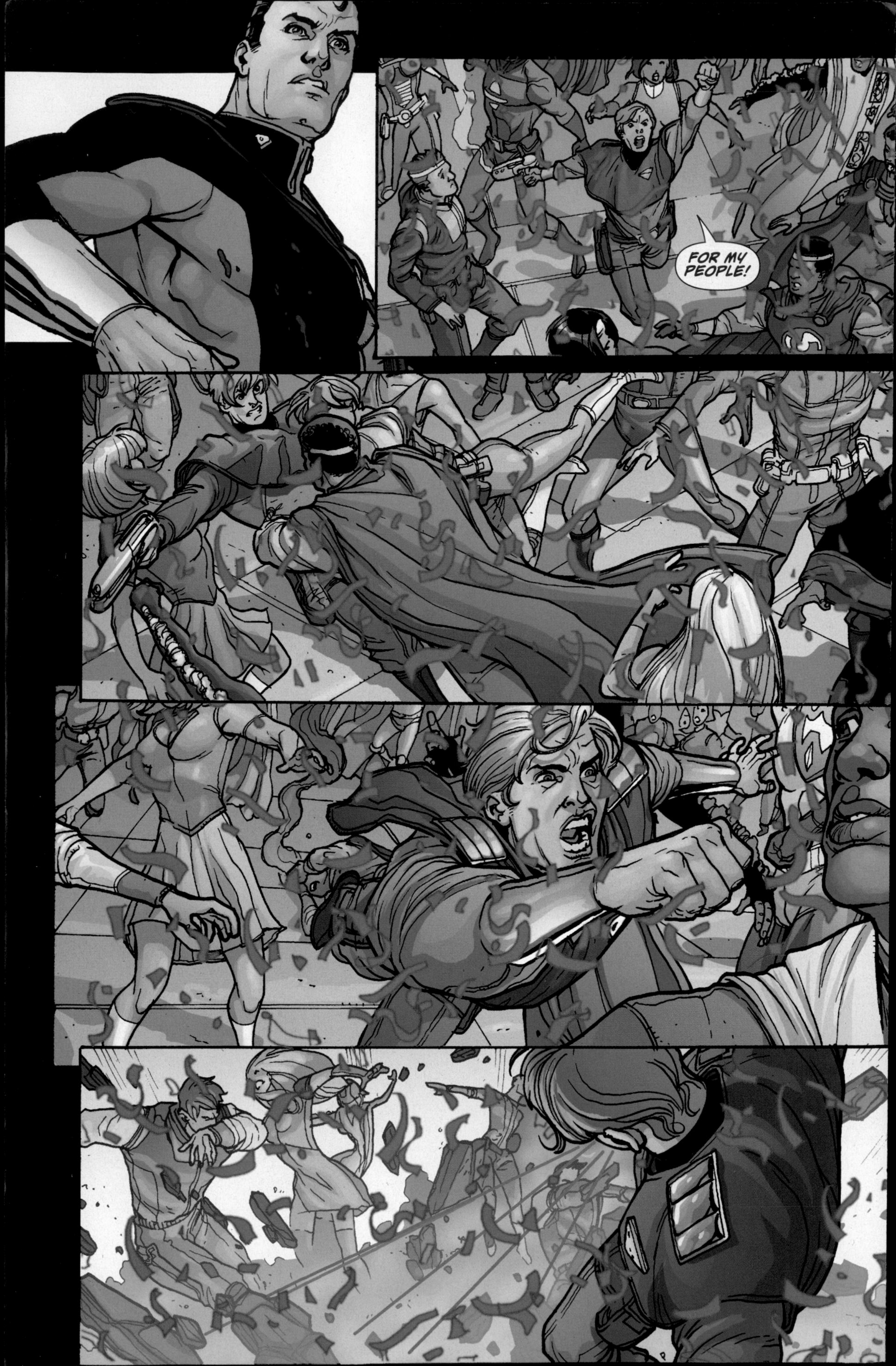
FOR MY PEOPLE!

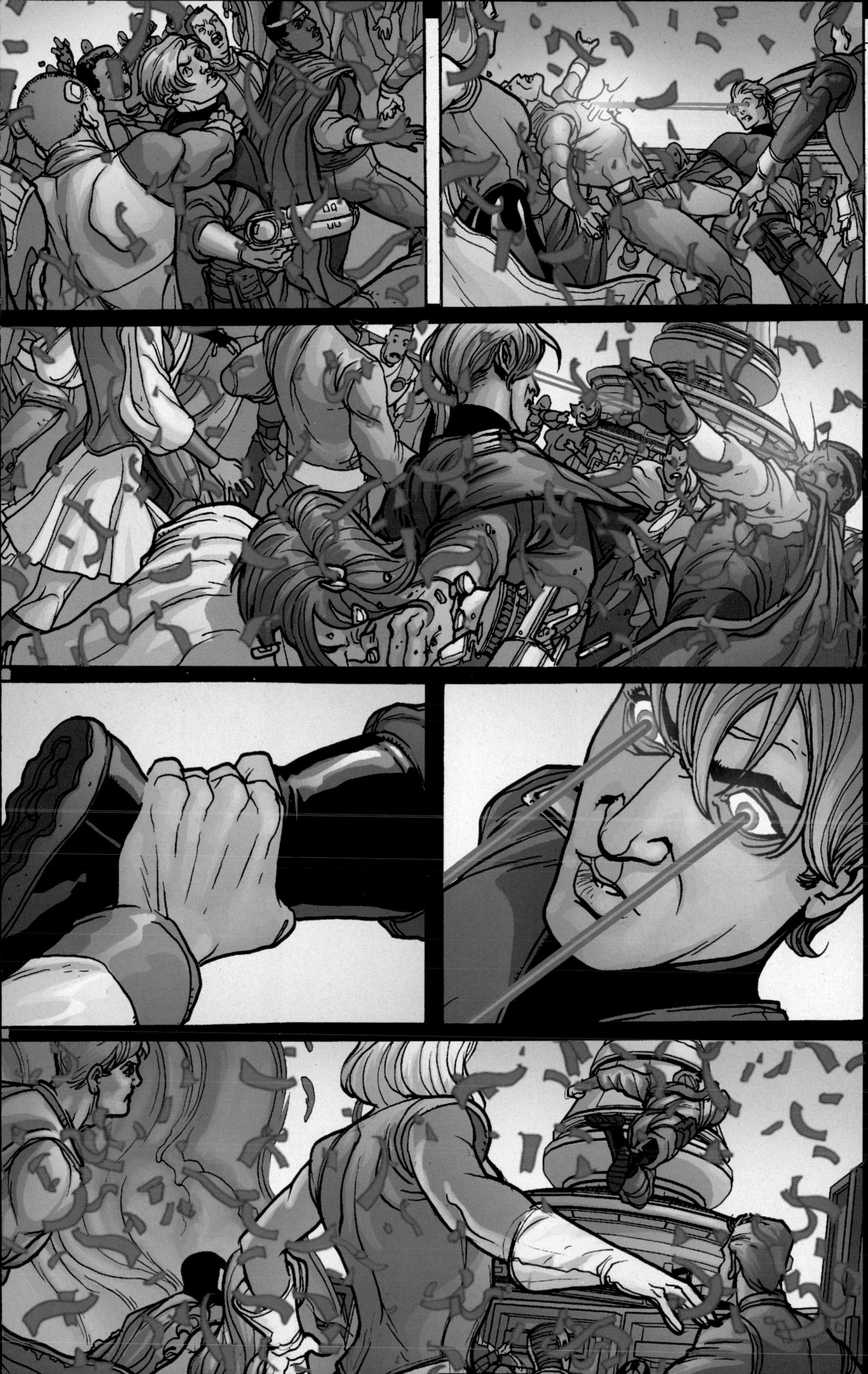

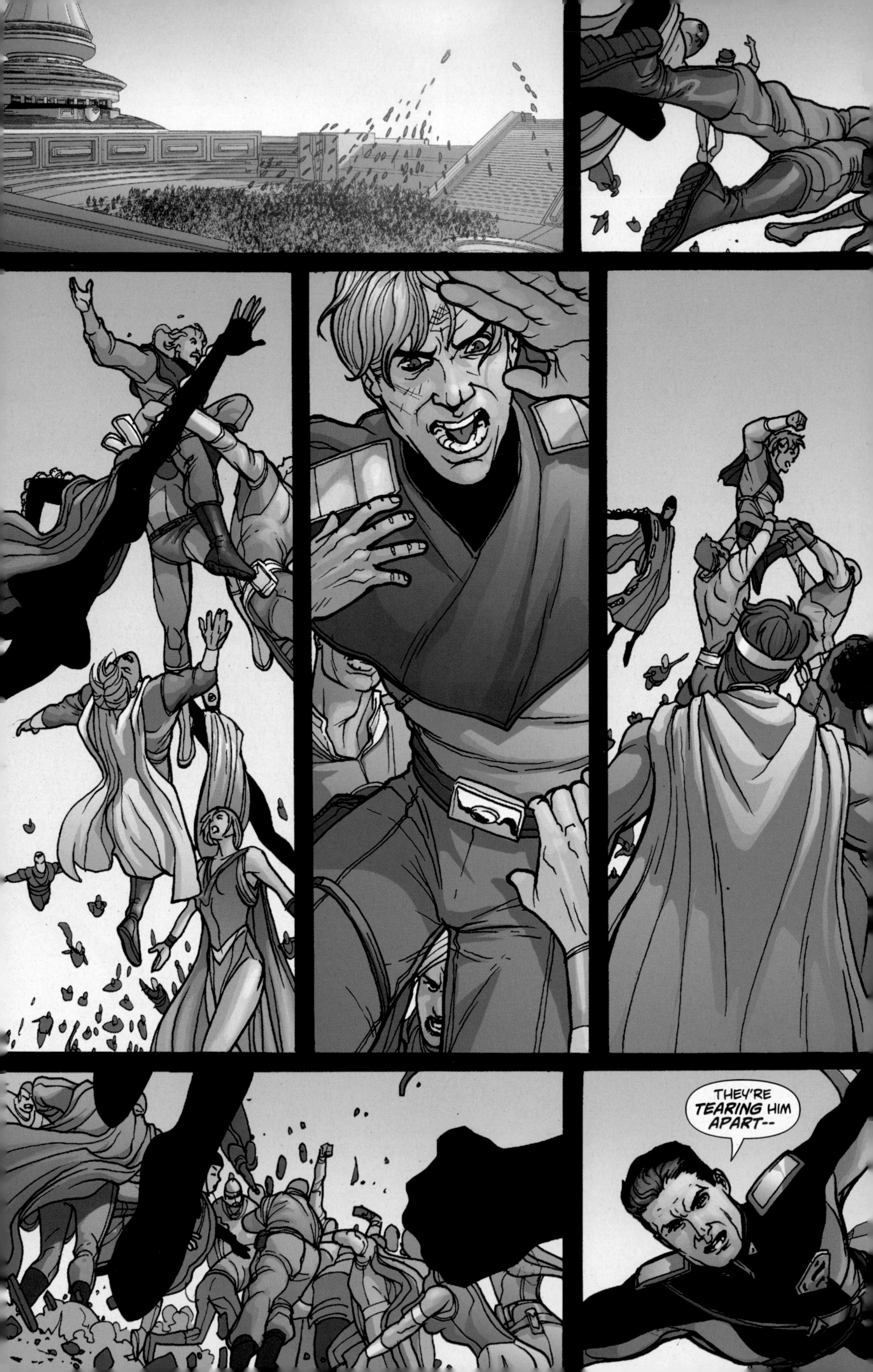
THEY'RE TEARING HIM APART--

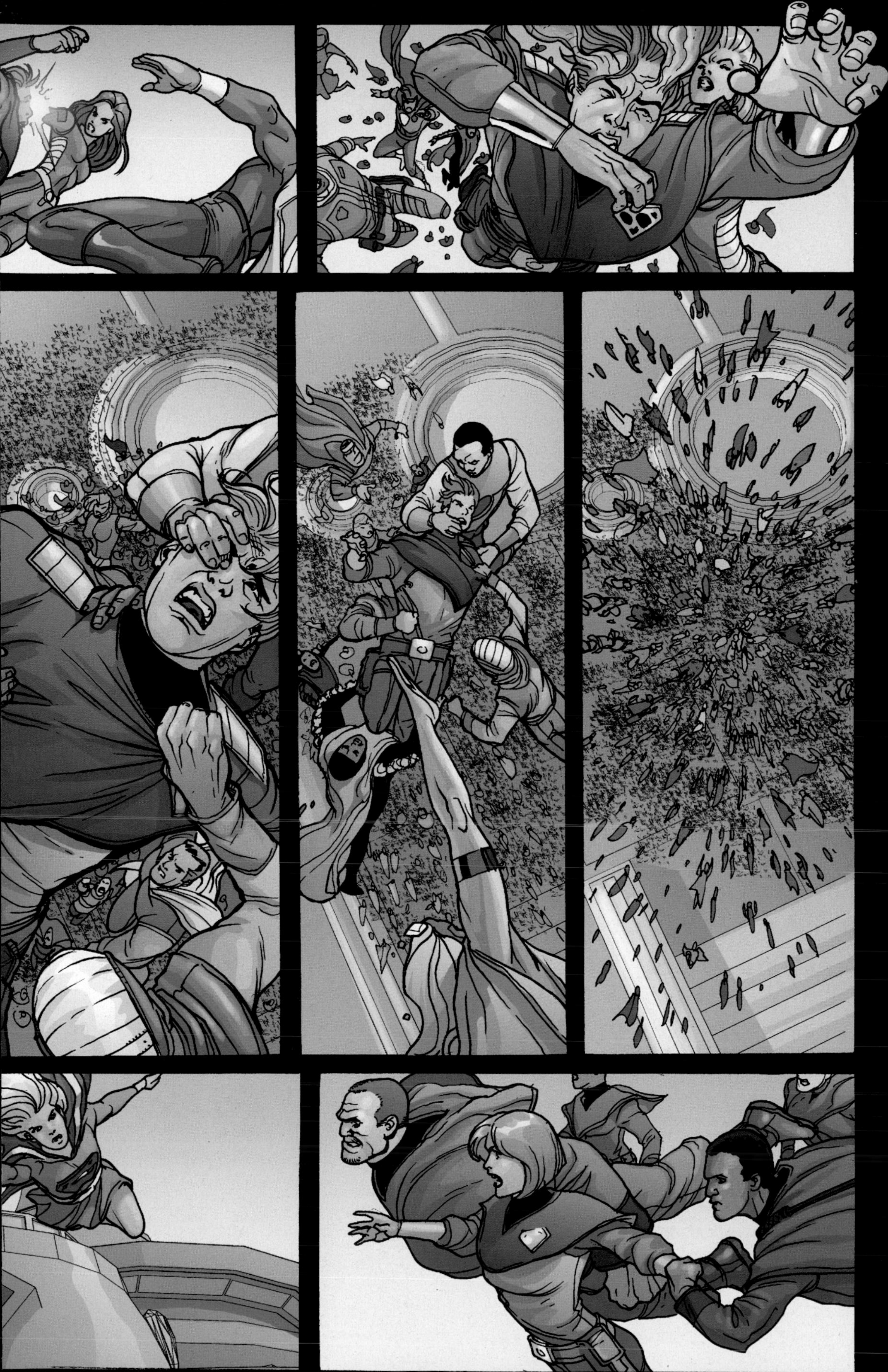

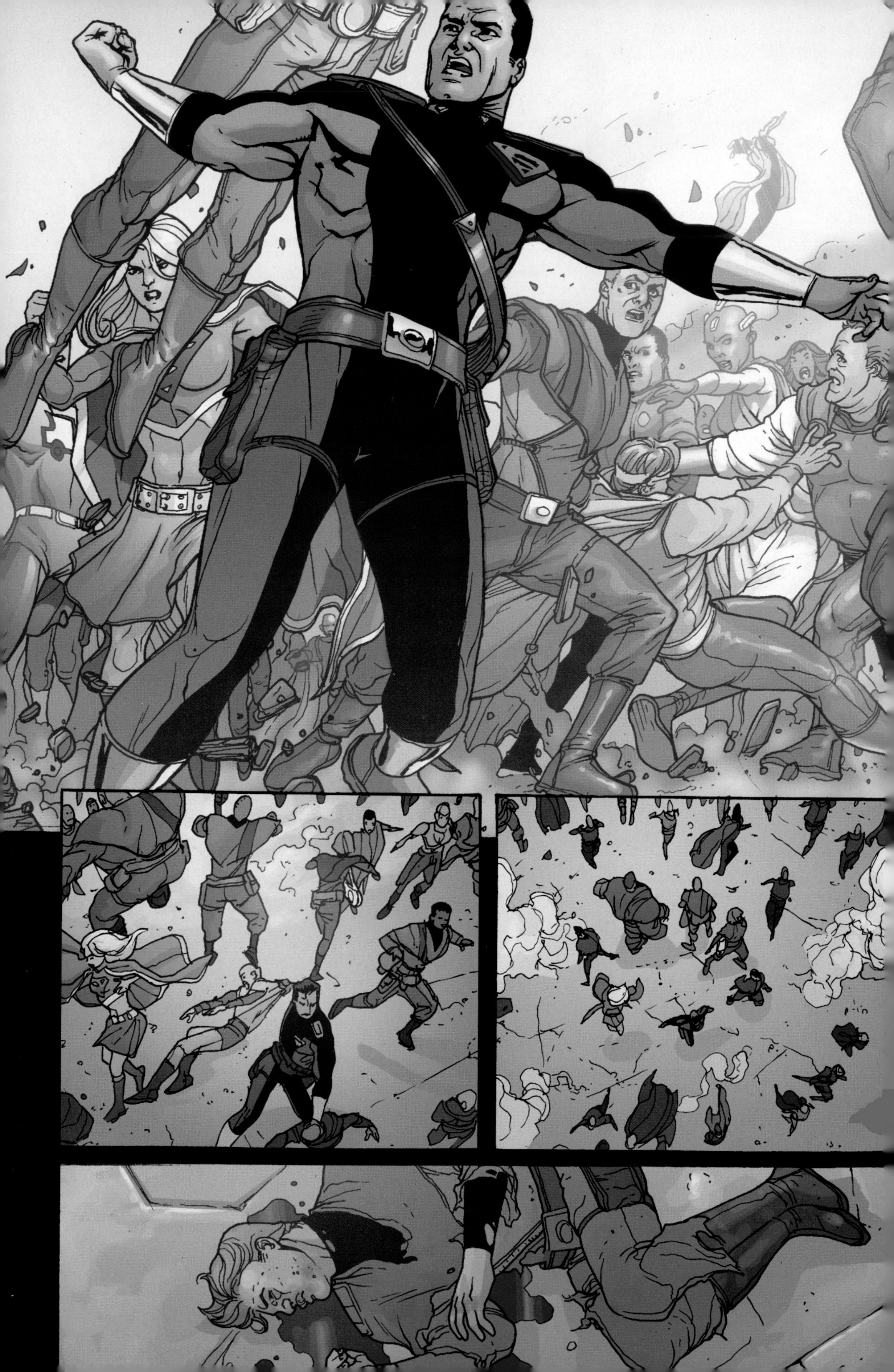

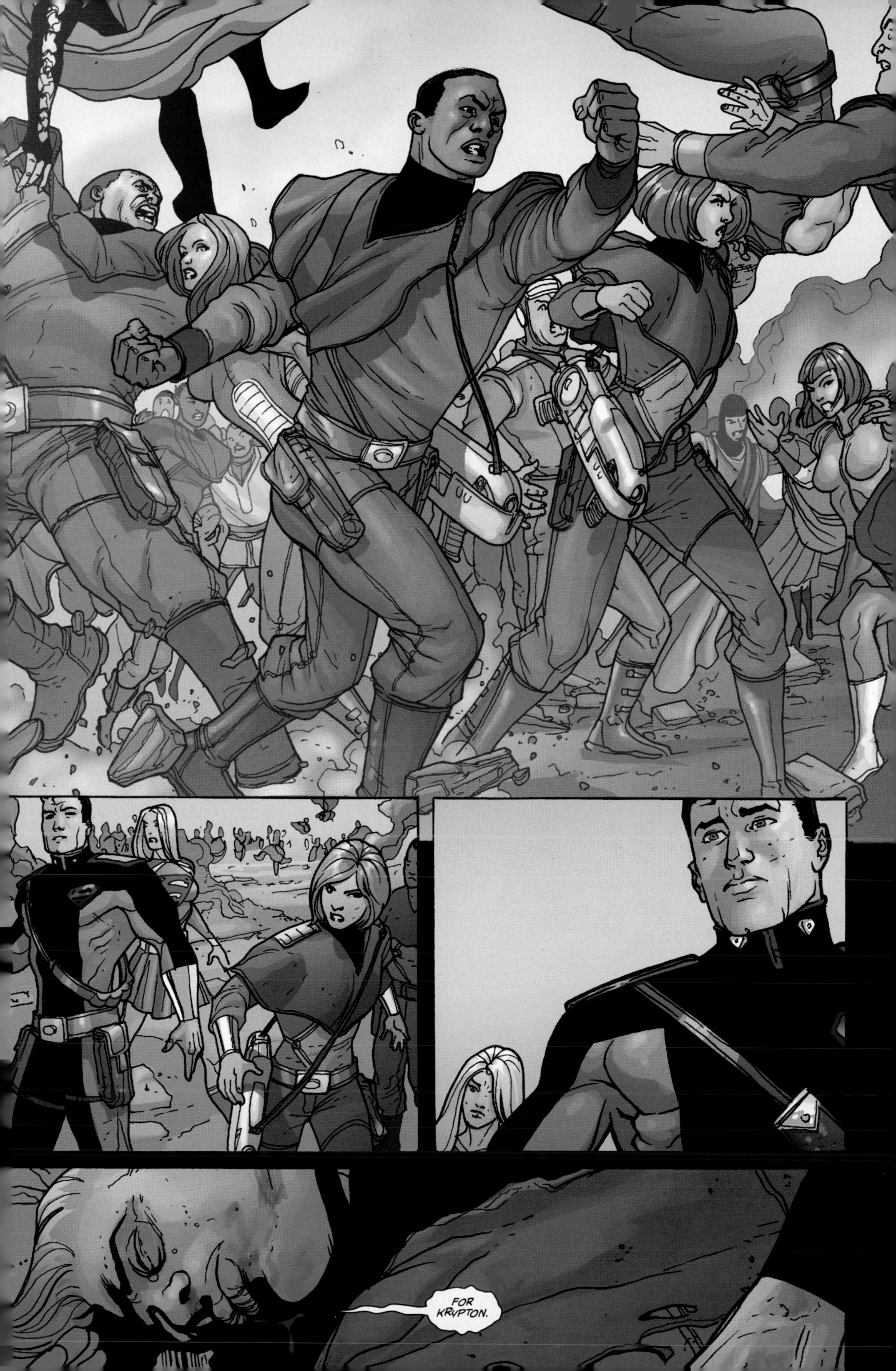
FOR KRYPTON.

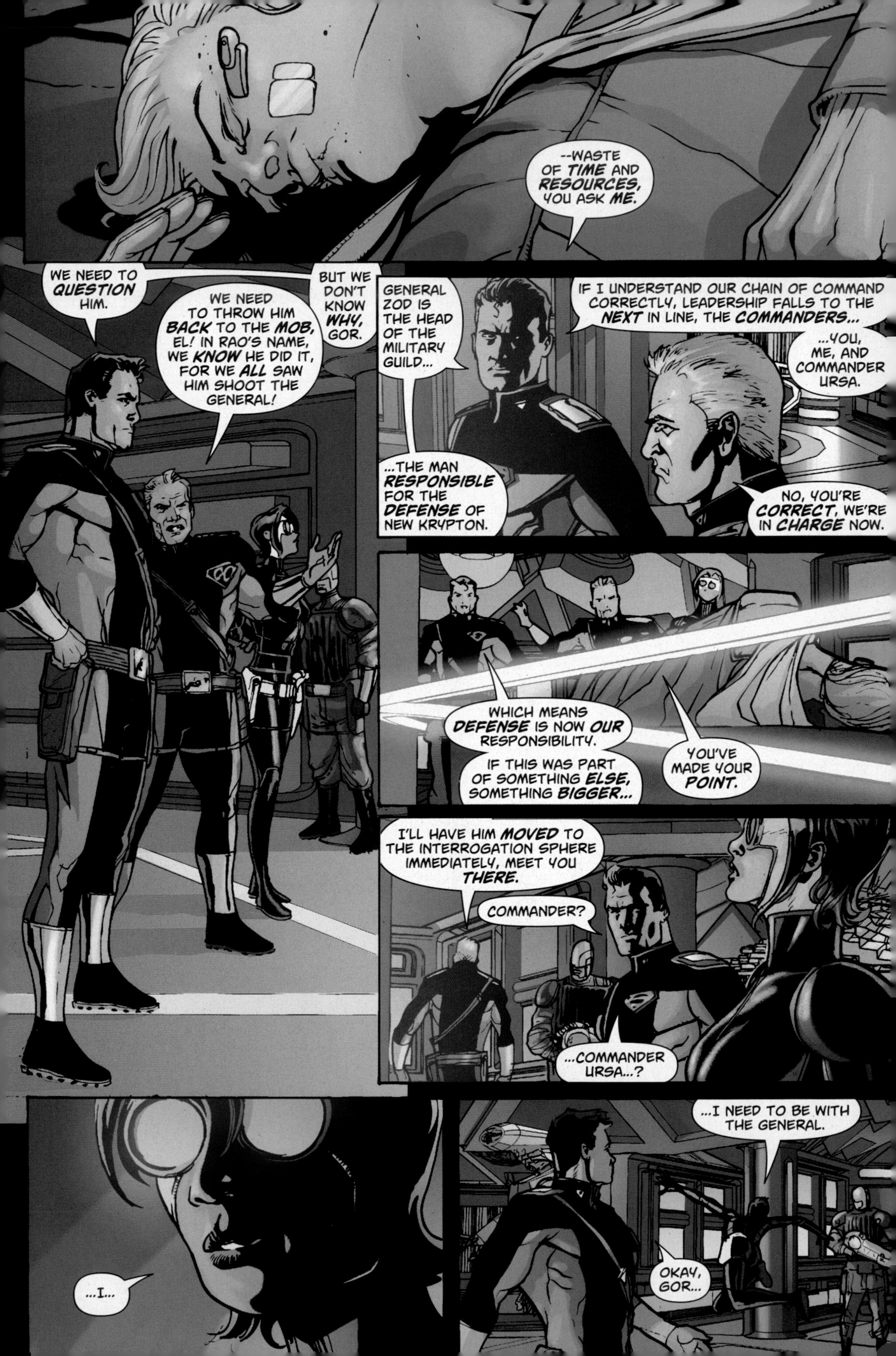
--WASTE OF TIME AND RESOURCES, YOU ASK ME.
WE NEED TO QUESTION HIM.
BUT WE DON'T KNOW WHY, GOR.
WE NEED TO THROW HIM BACK TO THE MOB, EL! IN RAO'S NAME, WE KNOW HE DID IT, FOR WE ALL SAW HIM SHOOT THE GENERAL!
GENERAL ZOD IS THE HEAD OF THE MILITARY GUILD...
...THE MAN RESPONSIBLE FOR THE DEFENSE OF NEW KRYPTON.
IF I UNDERSTAND OUR CHAIN OF COMMAND CORRECTLY, LEADERSHIP FALLS TO THE NEXT IN LINE, THE COMMANDERS...
...YOU, ME, AND COMMANDER URSA.
NO, YOU'RE CORRECT, WE'RE IN CHARGE NOW.
WHICH MEANS DEFENSE IS NOW OUR RESPONSIBILITY.
IF THIS WAS PART OF SOMETHING ELSE, SOMETHING BIGGER...
YOU'VE MADE YOUR POINT.
I'LL HAVE HIM MOVED TO THE INTERROGATION SPHERE IMMEDIATELY, MEET YOU THERE.
COMMANDER?
...COMMANDER URSA...?
...I...
...I NEED TO BE WITH THE GENERAL.
OKAY, GOR...

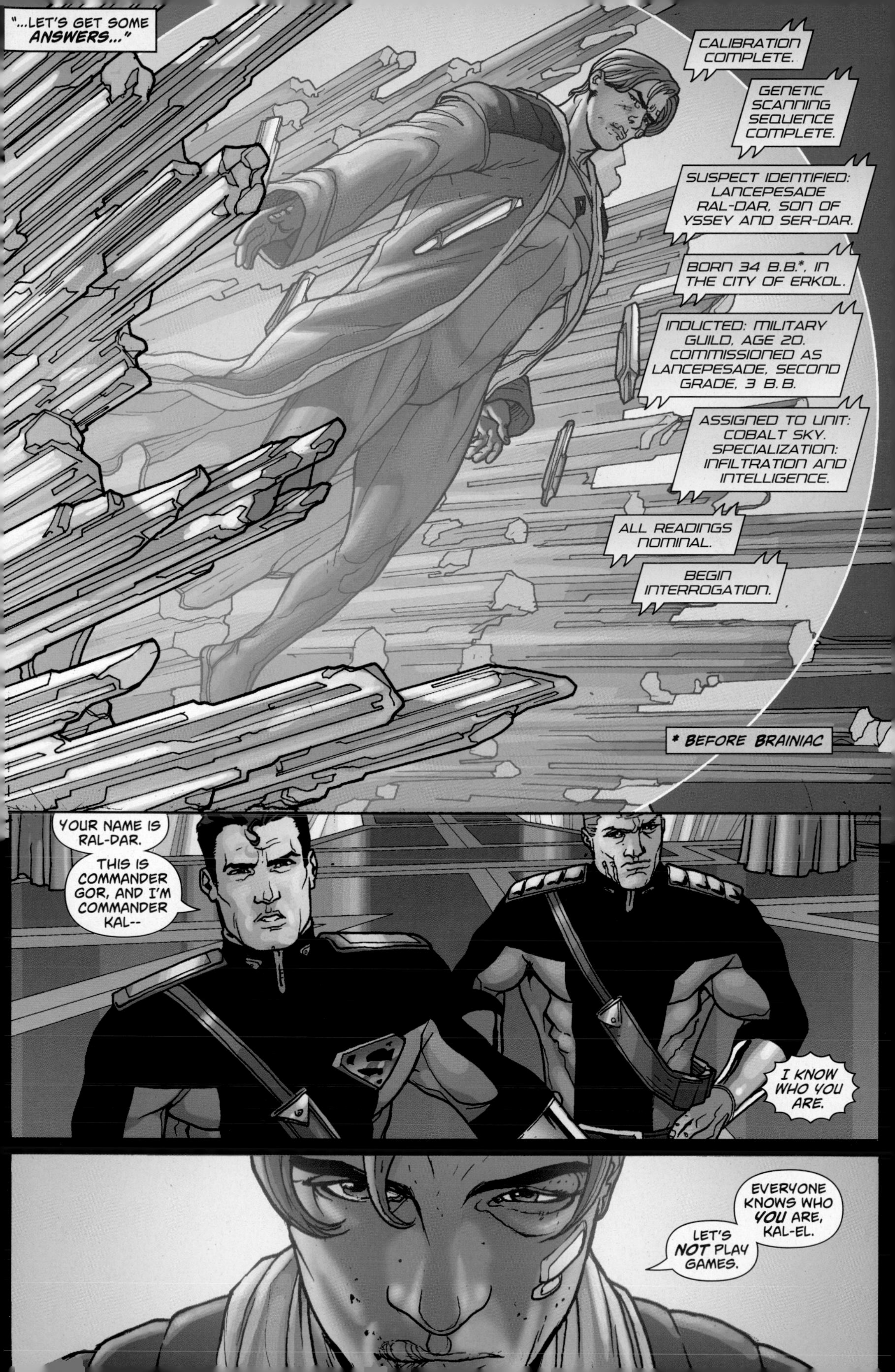
"...LET'S GET SOME ANSWERS..."
CALIBRATION COMPLETE.
GENETIC SCANNING SEQUENCE COMPLETE.
SUSPECT IDENTIFIED: LANCEPESADE RAL-DAR, SON OF YSSEY AND SER-DAR.
BORN 34 B.B.*, IN THE CITY OF ERKOL.
INDUCTED: MILITARY GUILD, AGE 20. COMMISSIONED AS LANCEPESADE, SECOND GRADE, 3 B.B.
ASSIGNED TO UNIT: COBALT SKY. SPECIALIZATION: INFILTRATION AND INTELLIGENCE.
ALL READINGS NOMINAL.
BEGIN INTERROGATION.
* BEFORE BRAINIAC
YOUR NAME IS RAL-DAR.
THIS IS COMMANDER GOR, AND I'M COMMANDER KAL--
I KNOW WHO YOU ARE.
EVERYONE KNOWS WHO YOU ARE, KAL-EL.
LET'S NOT PLAY GAMES.

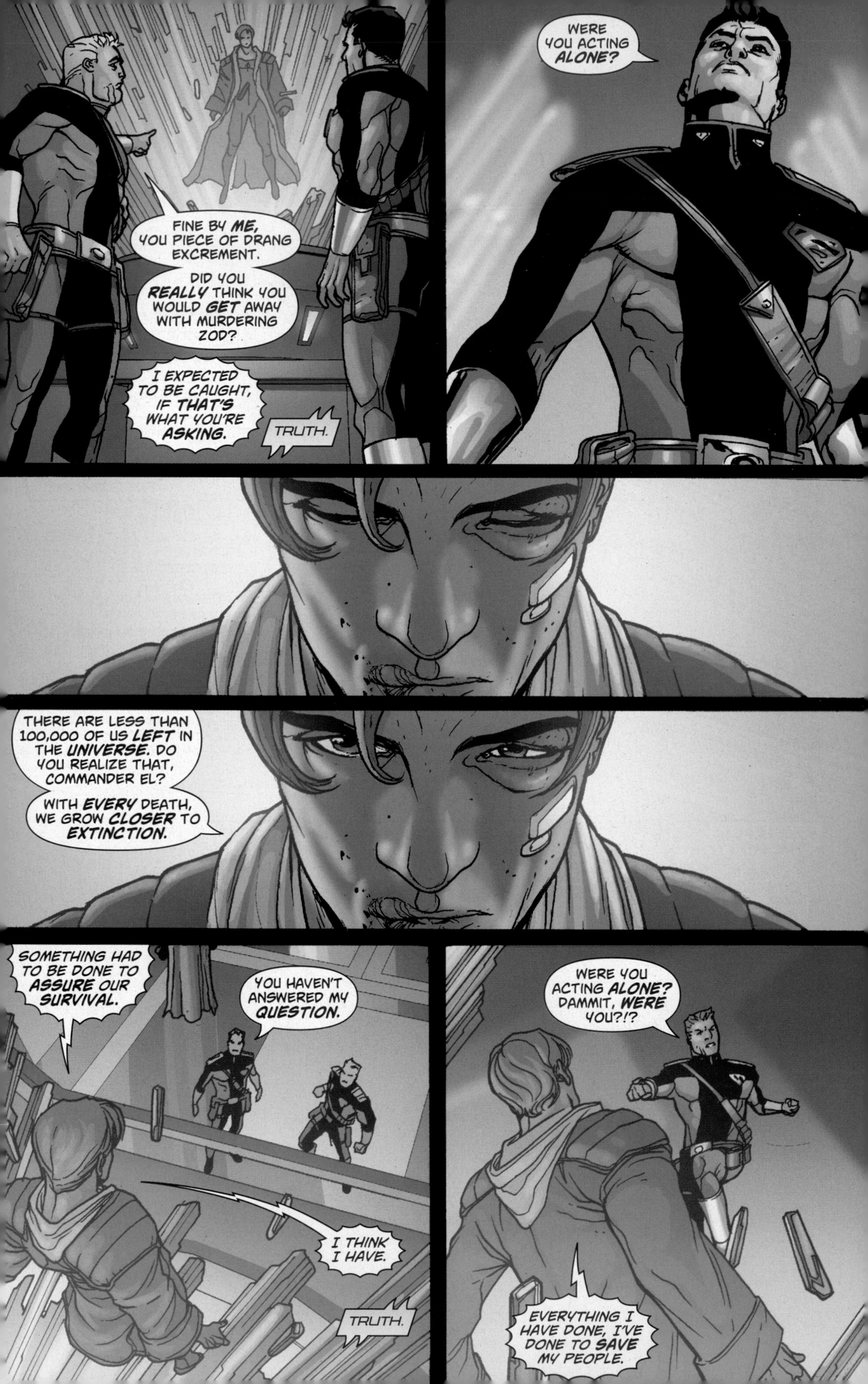
FINE BY ME, YOU PIECE OF DRANG EXCREMENT.
DID YOU REALLY THINK YOU WOULD GET AWAY WITH MURDERING ZOD?
I EXPECTED TO BE CAUGHT, IF THAT'S WHAT YOU'RE ASKING.
TRUTH.
WERE YOU ACTING ALONE?
THERE ARE LESS THAN 100,000 OF US LEFT IN THE UNIVERSE. DO YOU REALIZE THAT, COMMANDER EL?
WITH EVERY DEATH, WE GROW CLOSER TO EXTINCTION.
SOMETHING HAD TO BE DONE TO ASSURE OUR SURVIVAL.
YOU HAVEN'T ANSWERED MY QUESTION.
I THINK I HAVE.
TRUTH.
WERE YOU ACTING ALONE? DAMMIT, WERE YOU?!?
EVERYTHING I HAVE DONE, I'VE DONE TO SAVE MY PEOPLE.

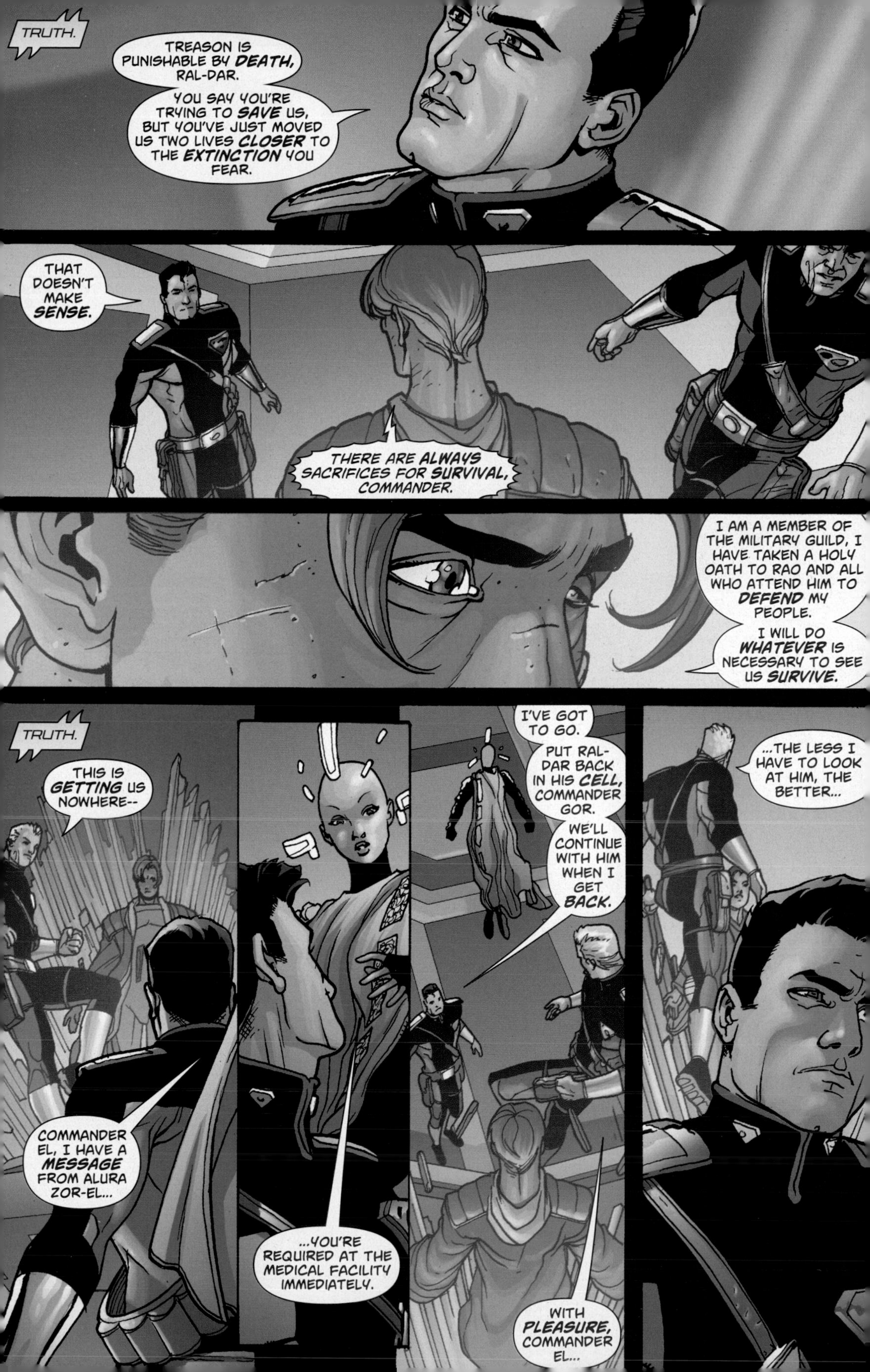
TRUTH.
TREASON IS PUNISHABLE BY DEATH, RAL-DAR.
YOU SAY YOU'RE TRYING TO SAVE US, BUT YOU'VE JUST MOVED US TWO LIVES CLOSER TO THE EXTINCTION YOU FEAR.
THAT DOESN'T MAKE SENSE.
THERE ARE ALWAYS SACRIFICES FOR SURVIVAL, COMMANDER.
I AM A MEMBER OF THE MILITARY GUILD, I HAVE TAKEN A HOLY OATH TO RAO AND ALL WHO ATTEND HIM TO DEFEND MY PEOPLE.
I WILL DO WHATEVER IS NECESSARY TO SEE US SURVIVE.
TRUTH.
THIS IS GETTING US NOWHERE--
COMMANDER EL, I HAVE A MESSAGE FROM ALURA ZOR-EL...
...YOU'RE REQUIRED AT THE MEDICAL FACILITY IMMEDIATELY.
I'VE GOT TO GO.
PUT RAL-DAR BACK IN HIS CELL, COMMANDER GOR.
WE'LL CONTINUE WITH HIM WHEN I GET BACK.
WITH PLEASURE, COMMANDER EL...
...THE LESS I HAVE TO LOOK AT HIM, THE BETTER...

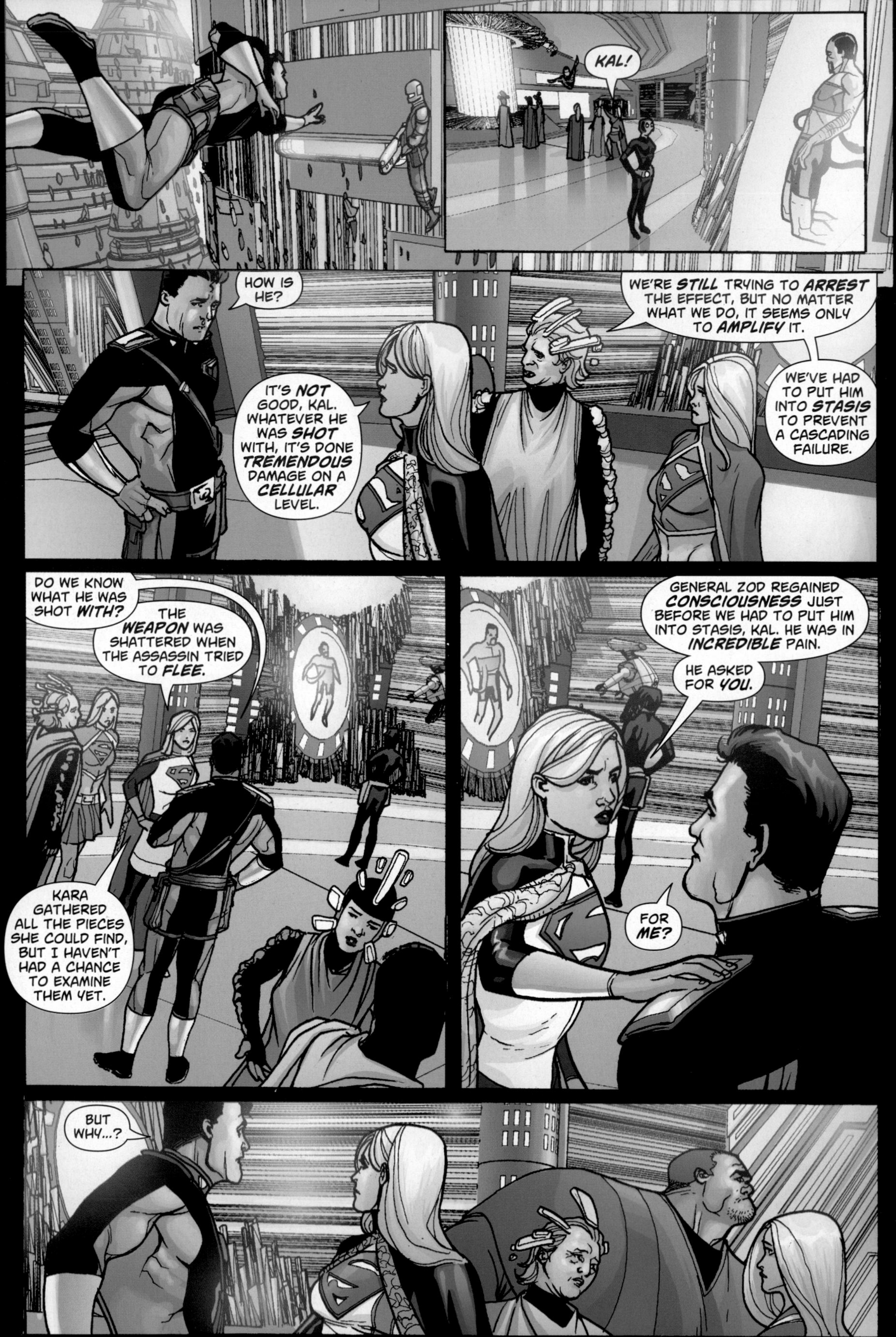
KAL!
HOW IS HE?
IT'S NOT GOOD, KAL. WHATEVER HE WAS SHOT WITH, IT'S DONE TREMENDOUS DAMAGE ON A CELLULAR LEVEL.
WE'RE STILL TRYING TO ARREST THE EFFECT, BUT NO MATTER WHAT WE DO, IT SEEMS ONLY TO AMPLIFY IT.
WE'VE HAD TO PUT HIM INTO STASIS TO PREVENT A CASCADING FAILURE.
DO WE KNOW WHAT HE WAS SHOT WITH?
THE WEAPON WAS SHATTERED WHEN THE ASSASSIN TRIED TO FLEE.
KARA GATHERED ALL THE PIECES SHE COULD FIND, BUT I HAVEN'T HAD A CHANCE TO EXAMINE THEM YET.
GENERAL ZOD REGAINED CONSCIOUSNESS JUST BEFORE WE HAD TO PUT HIM INTO STASIS, KAL. HE WAS IN INCREDIBLE PAIN.
HE ASKED FOR YOU.
FOR ME?
BUT WHY...?

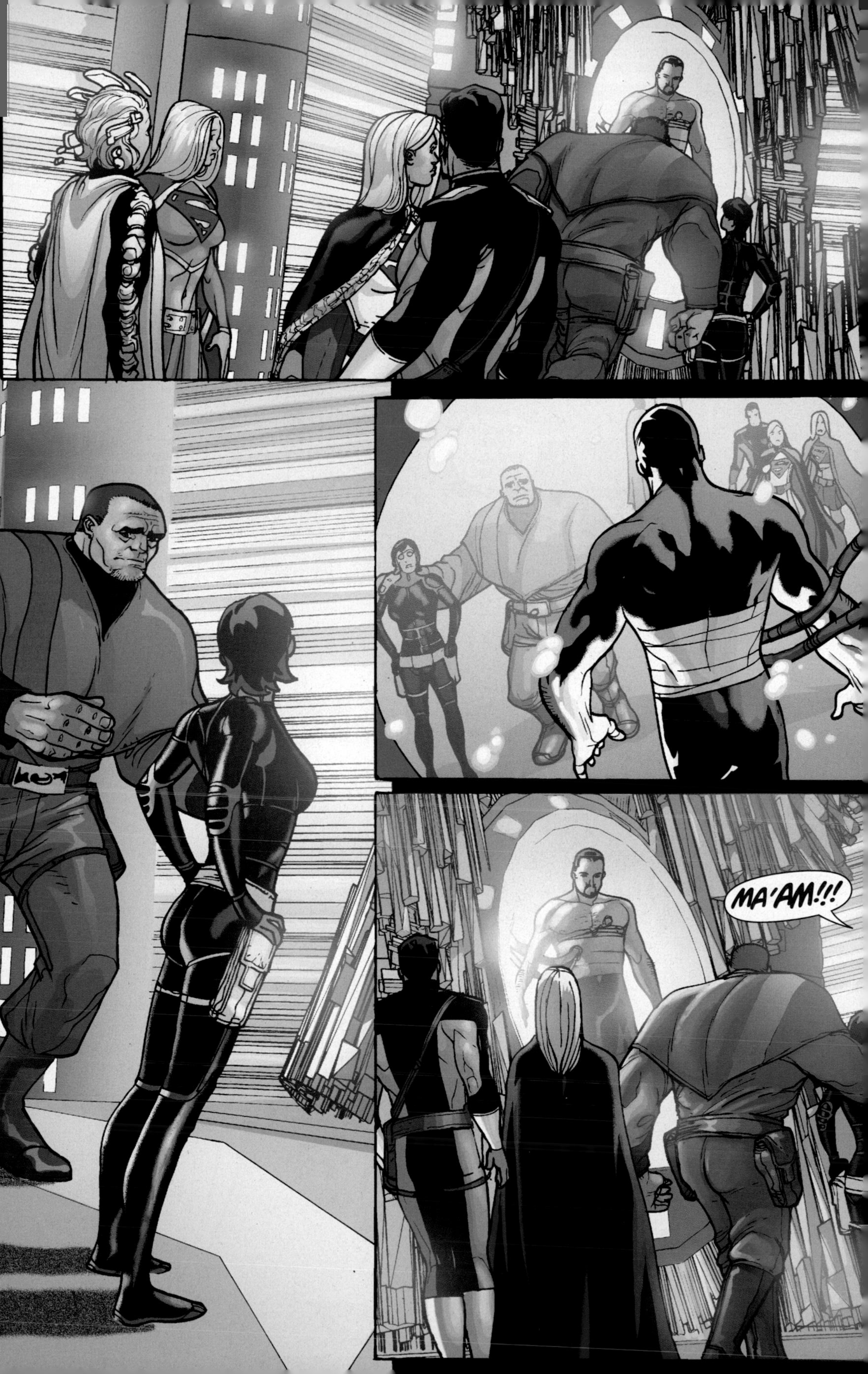
MA'AM!!!

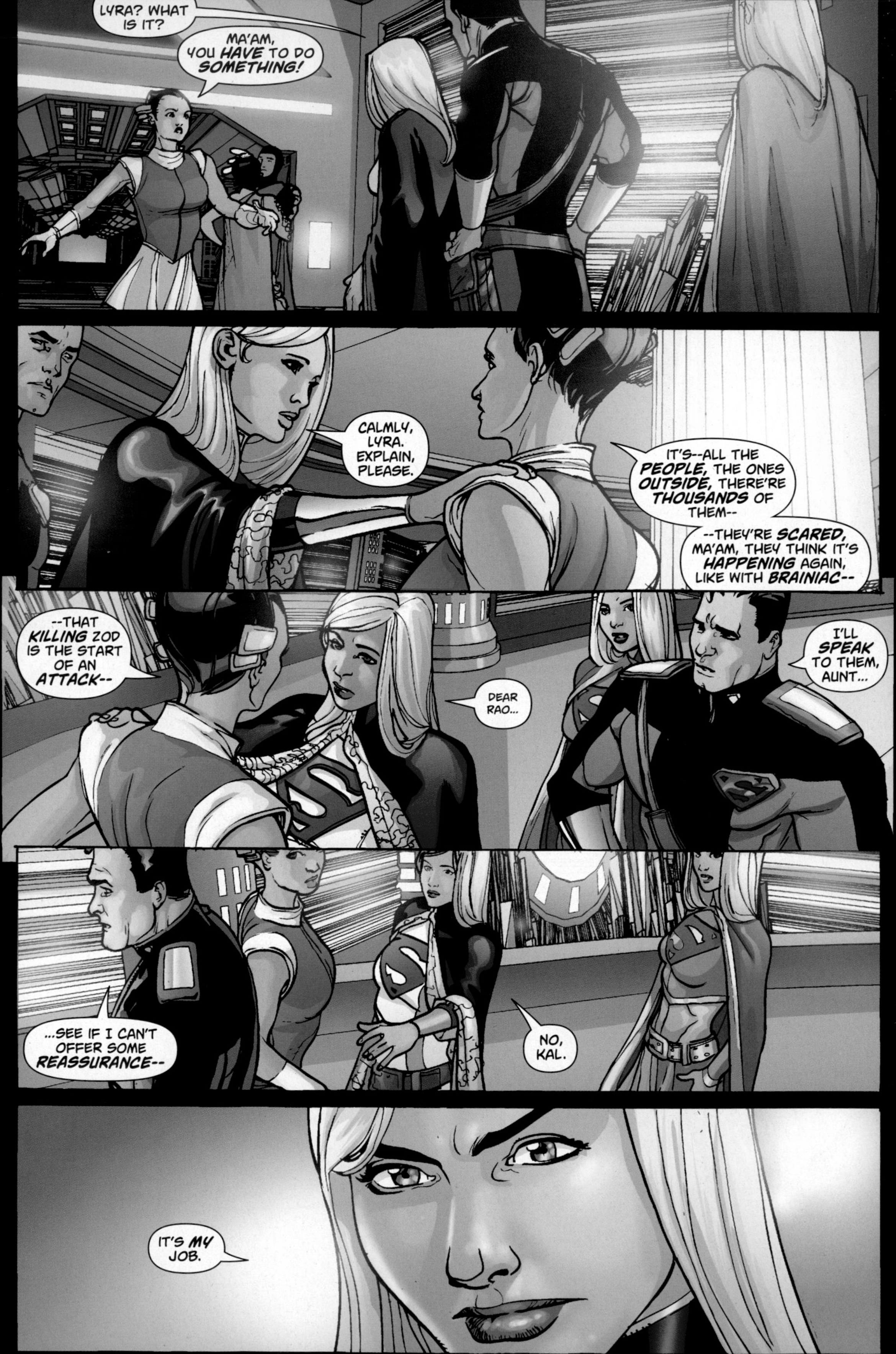
LYRA? WHAT IS IT?
MA'AM, YOU HAVE TO DO SOMETHING!
CALMLY, LYRA. EXPLAIN, PLEASE.
IT'S--ALL THE PEOPLE, THE ONES OUTSIDE, THERE'RE THOUSANDS OF THEM--
--THEY'RE SCARED, MA'AM, THEY THINK IT'S HAPPENING AGAIN, LIKE WITH BRAINIAC--
--THAT KILLING ZOD IS THE START OF AN ATTACK--
DEAR RAO...
I'LL SPEAK TO THEM, AUNT...
...SEE IF I CAN'T OFFER SOME REASSURANCE--
NO, KAL.
IT'S MY JOB.

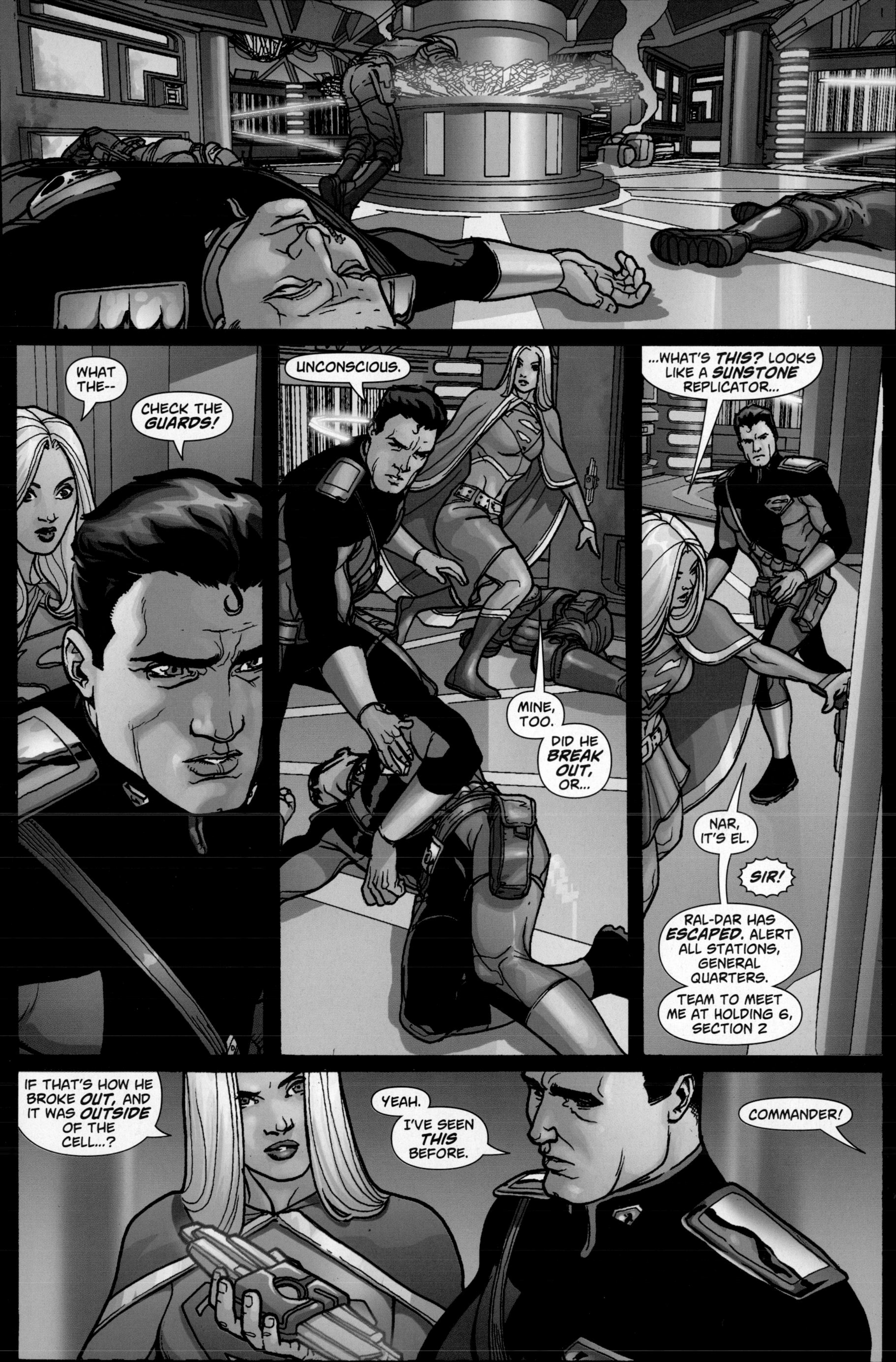
WHAT THE--
CHECK THE GUARDS!
UNCONSCIOUS.
MINE, TOO.
DID HE BREAK OUT, OR...
...WHAT'S THIS? LOOKS LIKE A SUNSTONE REPLICATOR...
NAR, IT'S EL.
SIR!
RAL-DAR HAS ESCAPED. ALERT ALL STATIONS, GENERAL QUARTERS.
TEAM TO MEET ME AT HOLDING 6, SECTION 2
IF THAT'S HOW HE BROKE OUT, AND IT WAS OUTSIDE OF THE CELL...?
YEAH.
I'VE SEEN THIS BEFORE.
COMMANDER!

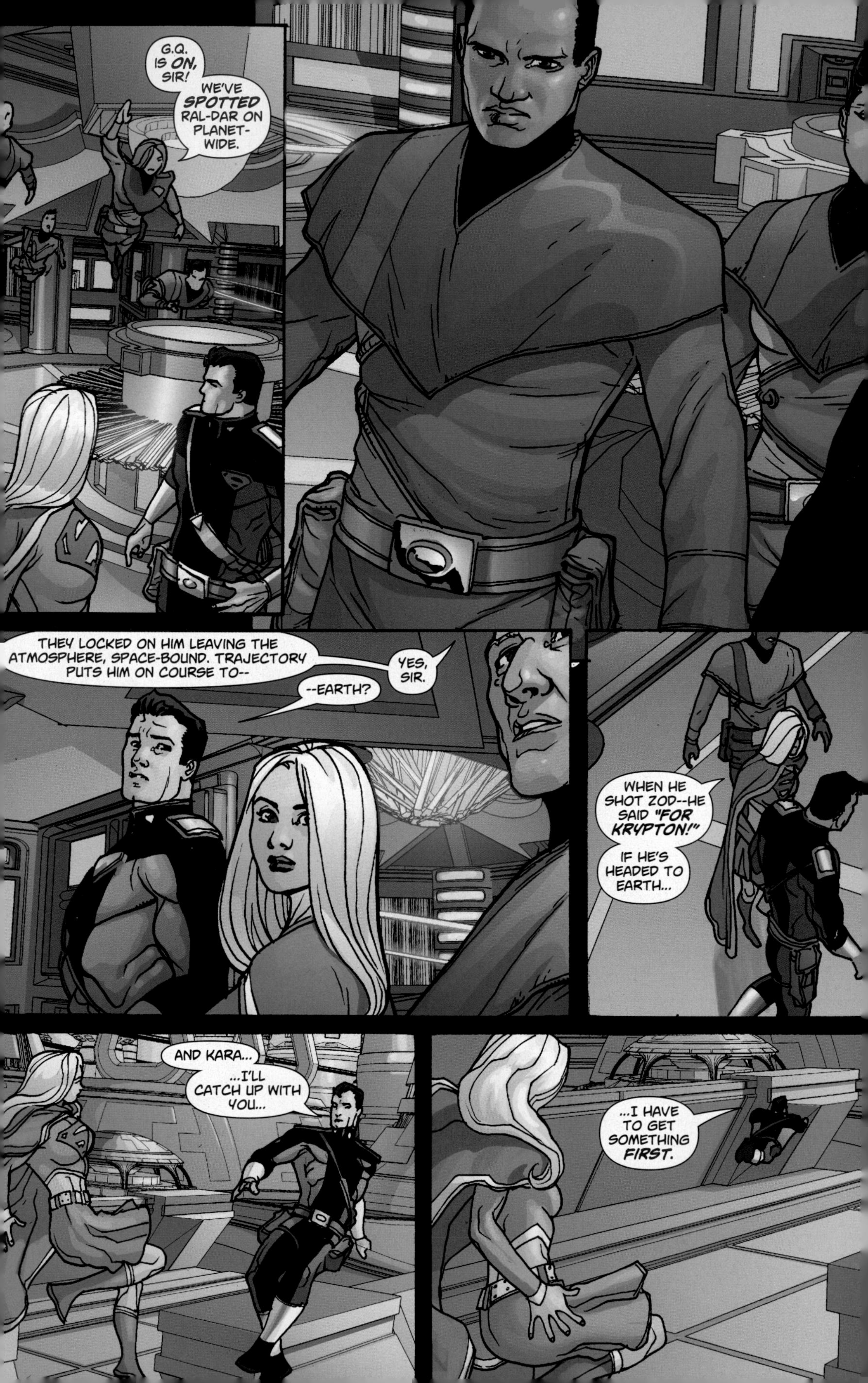
G.Q. IS ON, SIR!
WE'VE SPOTTED RAL-DAR ON PLANET-WIDE.
THEY LOCKED ON HIM LEAVING THE ATMOSPHERE, SPACE-BOUND. TRAJECTORY PUTS HIM ON COURSE TO--
--EARTH?
YES, SIR.
WHEN HE SHOT ZOD--HE SAID "FOR KRYPTON!"
IF HE'S HEADED TO EARTH...
AND KARA...
...I'LL CATCH UP WITH YOU...
...I HAVE TO GET SOMETHING FIRST.

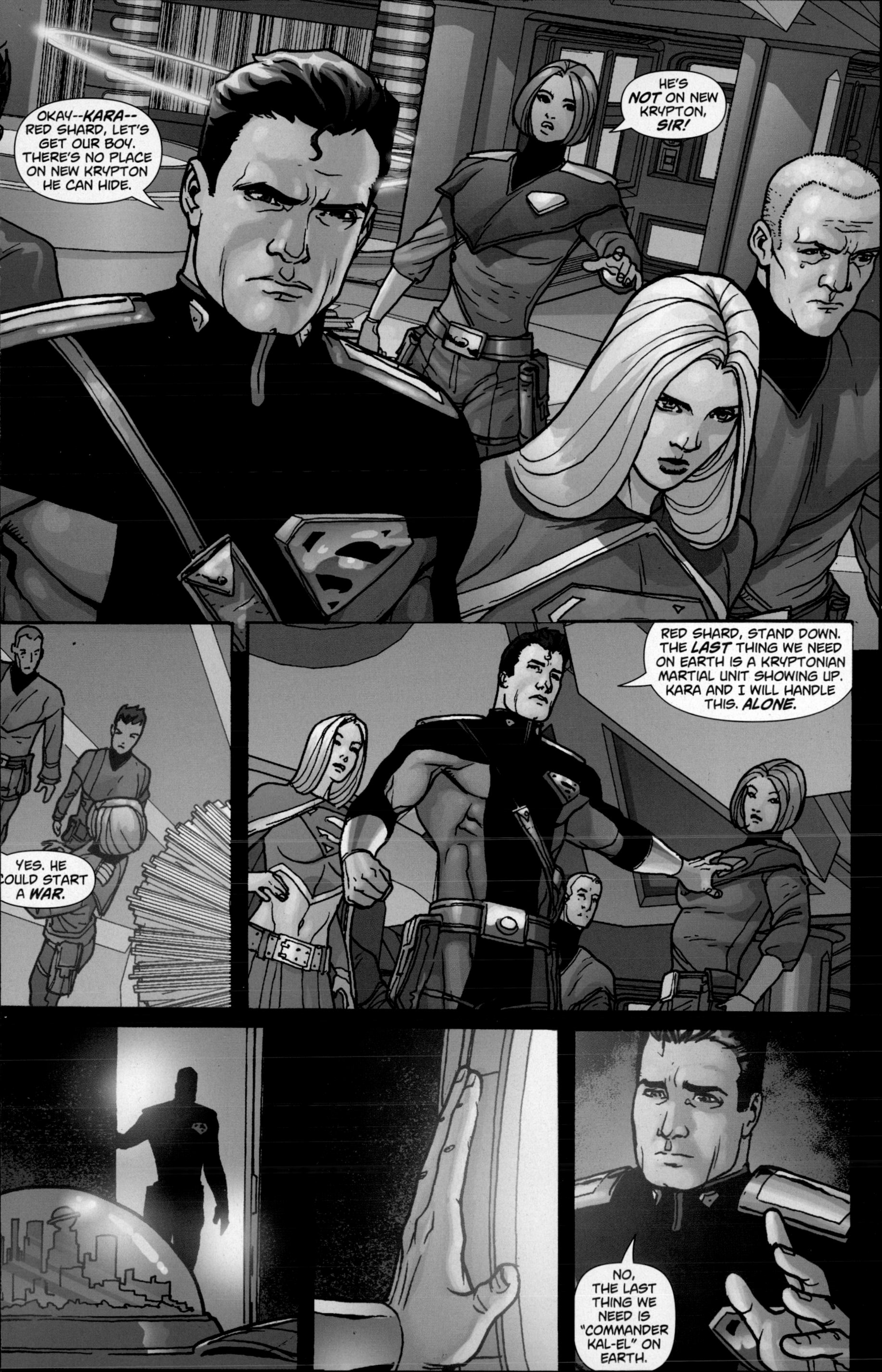
OKAY--KARA--RED SHARD, LET'S GET OUR BOY. THERE'S NO PLACE ON NEW KRYPTON HE CAN HIDE.
HE'S NOT ON NEW KRYPTON, SIR!
YES. HE COULD START A WAR.
RED SHARD, STAND DOWN. THE LAST THING WE NEED ON EARTH IS A KRYPTONIAN MARTIAL UNIT SHOWING UP. KARA AND I WILL HANDLE THIS. ALONE.
NO, THE LAST THING WE NEED IS "COMMANDER KAL-EL" ON EARTH.

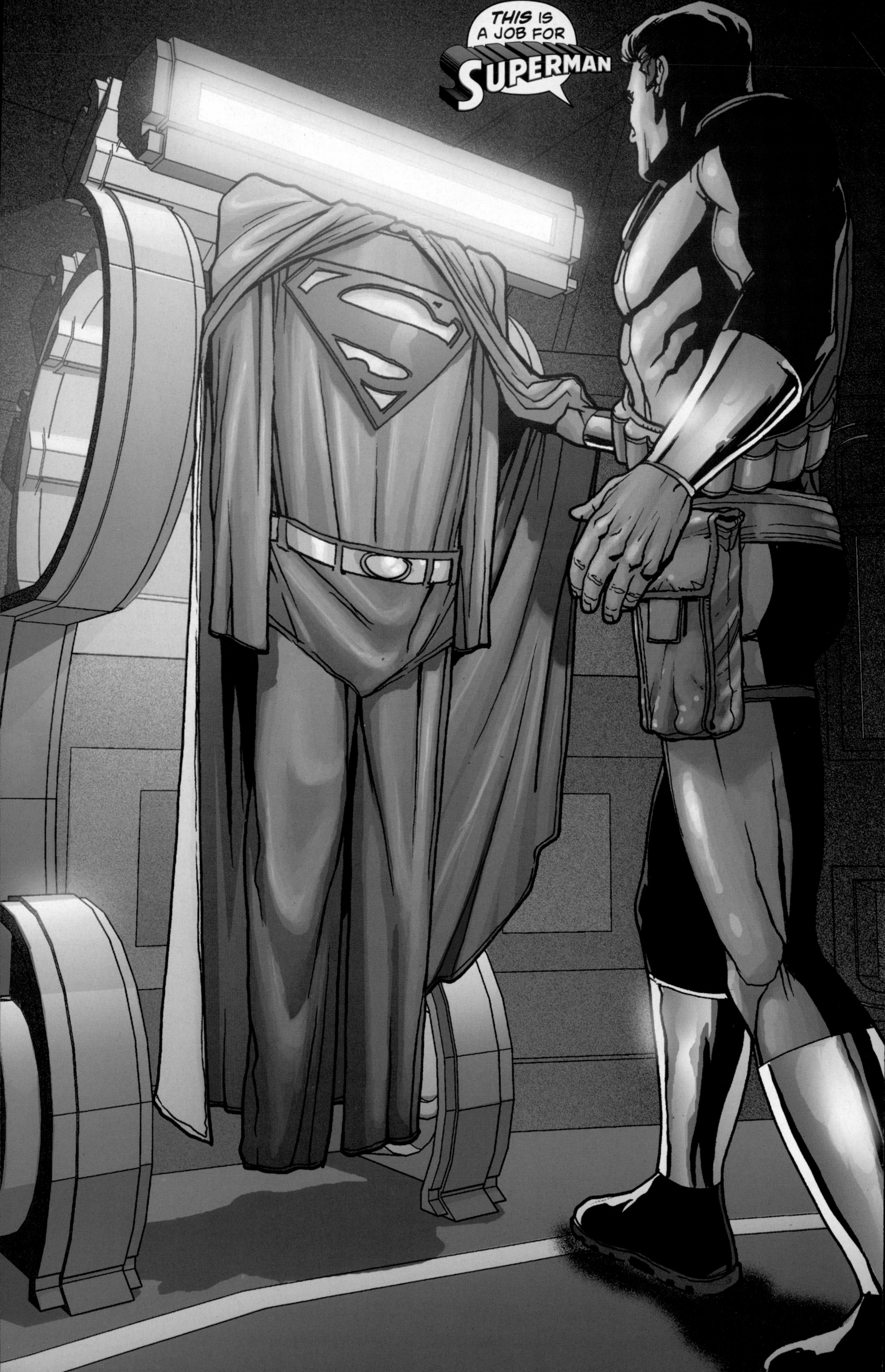
THIS IS A JOB FOR SUPERMAN

<ACTION COMICS 880>

COVER ART BY **FERNANDO DAGNINO** & **RAÚL FERNANDEZ** WITH **MAZI**

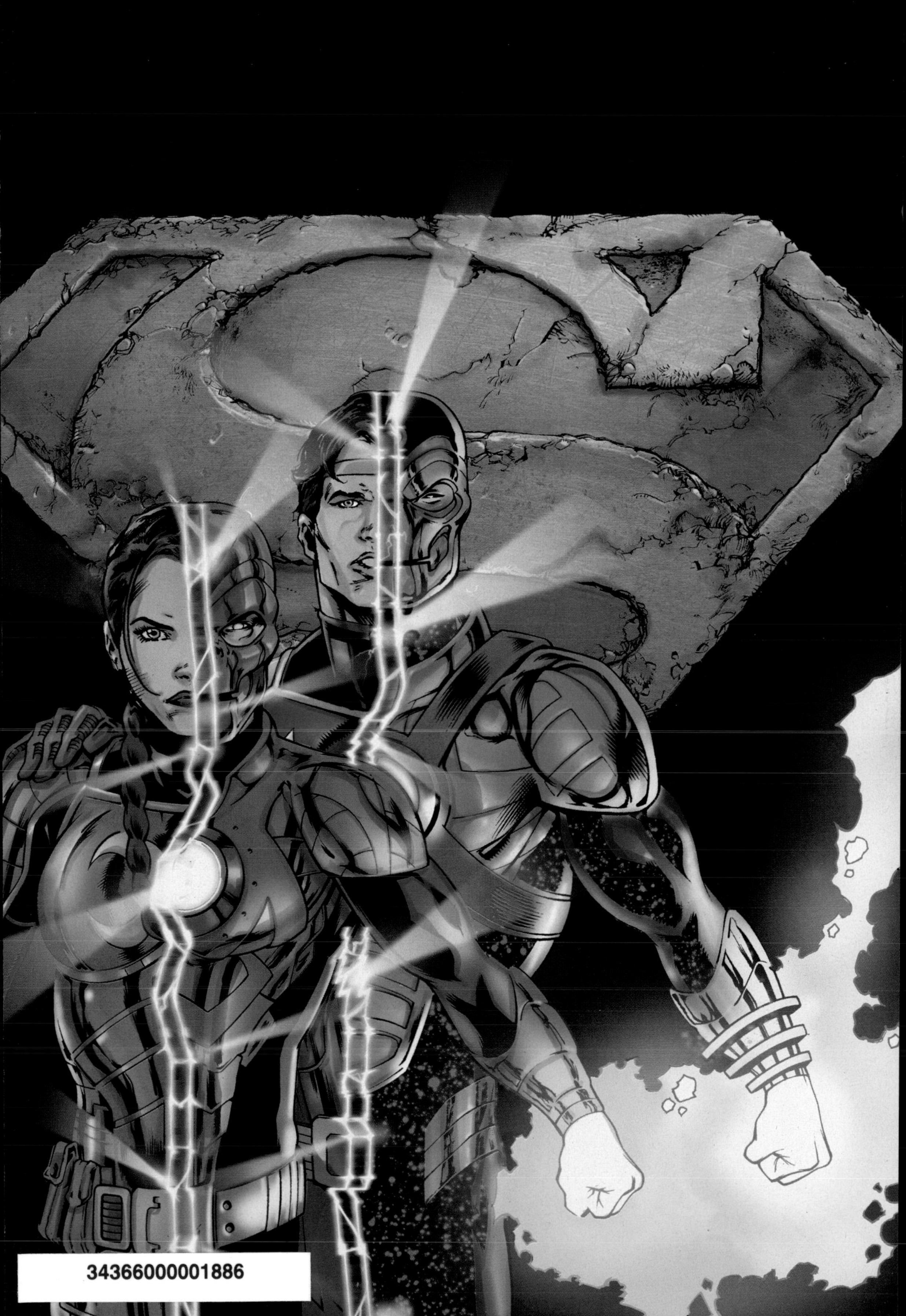

CODENAME: PATRIOT <PART TWO>

GREG RUCKA & JAMES ROBINSON – WRITERS
JULIÁN LÓPEZ – PENCILLER
BIT – INKER

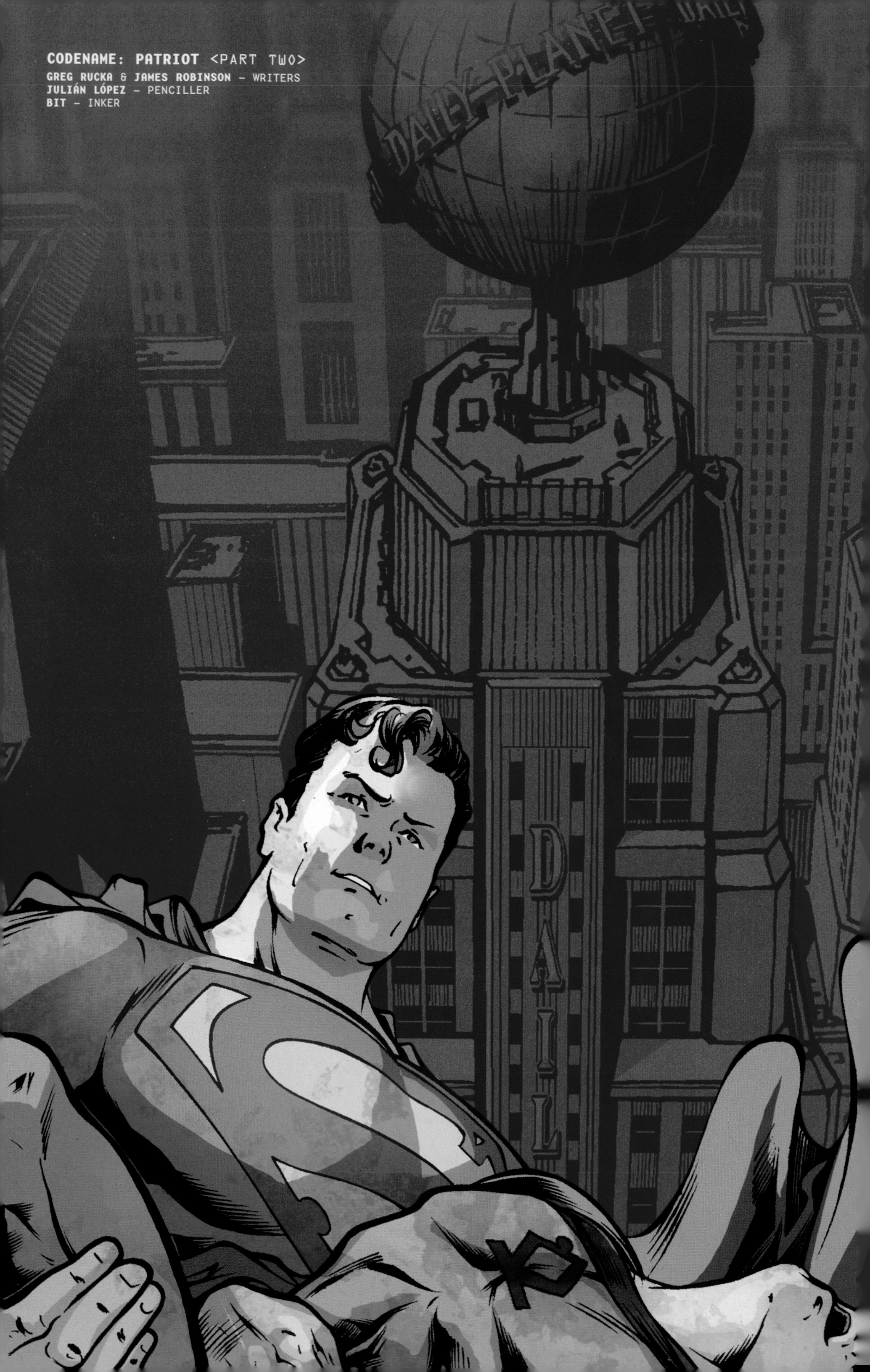

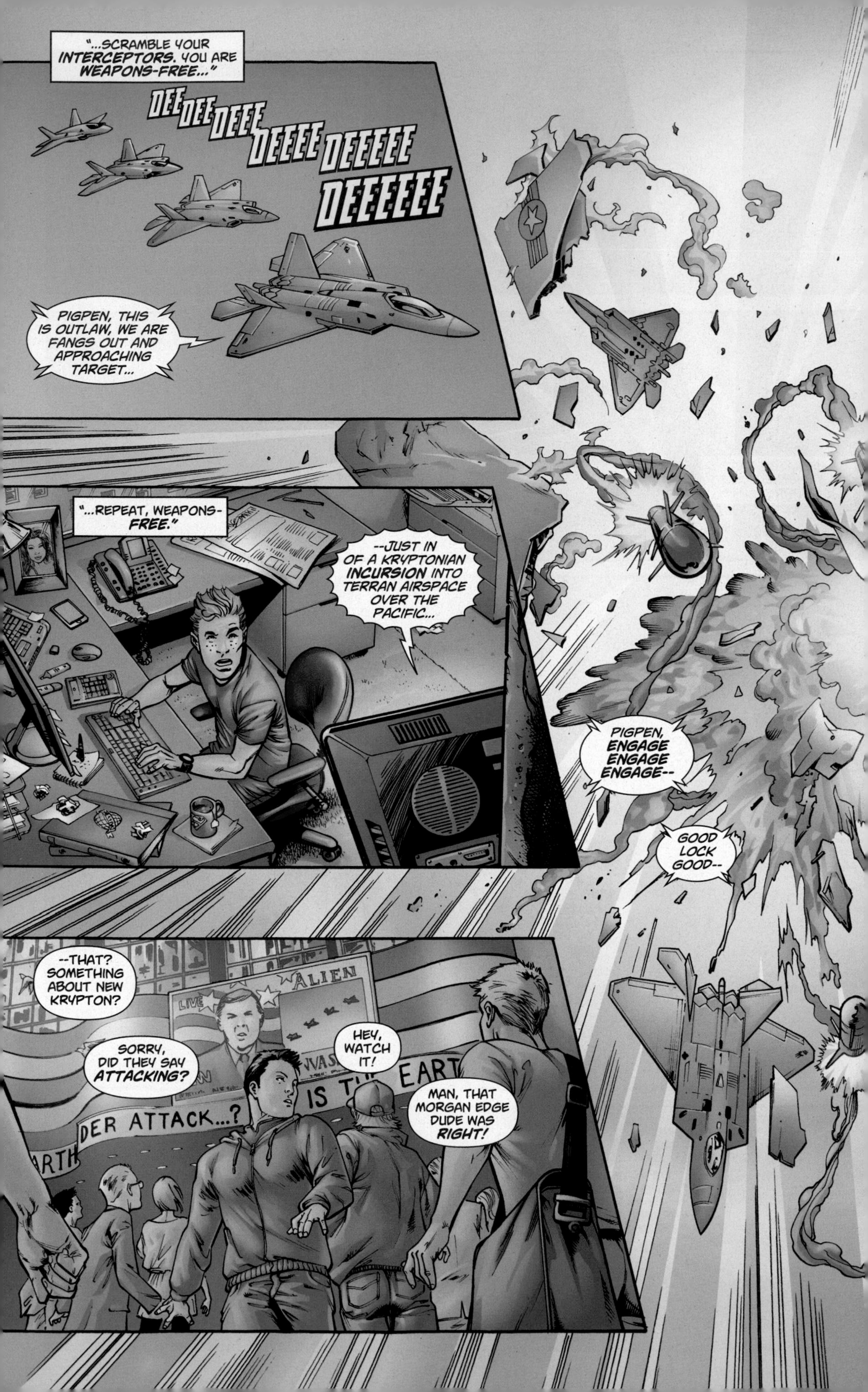
"...SCRAMBLE YOUR INTERCEPTORS. YOU ARE WEAPONS-FREE..."
DEE DEE DEEE DEEEE DEEEEE DEEEEEE
PIGPEN, THIS IS OUTLAW, WE ARE FANGS OUT AND APPROACHING TARGET...
"...REPEAT, WEAPONS-FREE."
--JUST IN OF A KRYPTONIAN INCURSION INTO TERRAN AIRSPACE OVER THE PACIFIC...
PIGPEN, ENGAGE ENGAGE ENGAGE--
GOOD LOCK GOOD--
--THAT? SOMETHING ABOUT NEW KRYPTON?
SORRY, DID THEY SAY ATTACKING?
HEY, WATCH IT!
MAN, THAT MORGAN EDGE DUDE WAS RIGHT!
LIVE
ALIEN
DER ATTACK...?
IS TH EART
ARTH

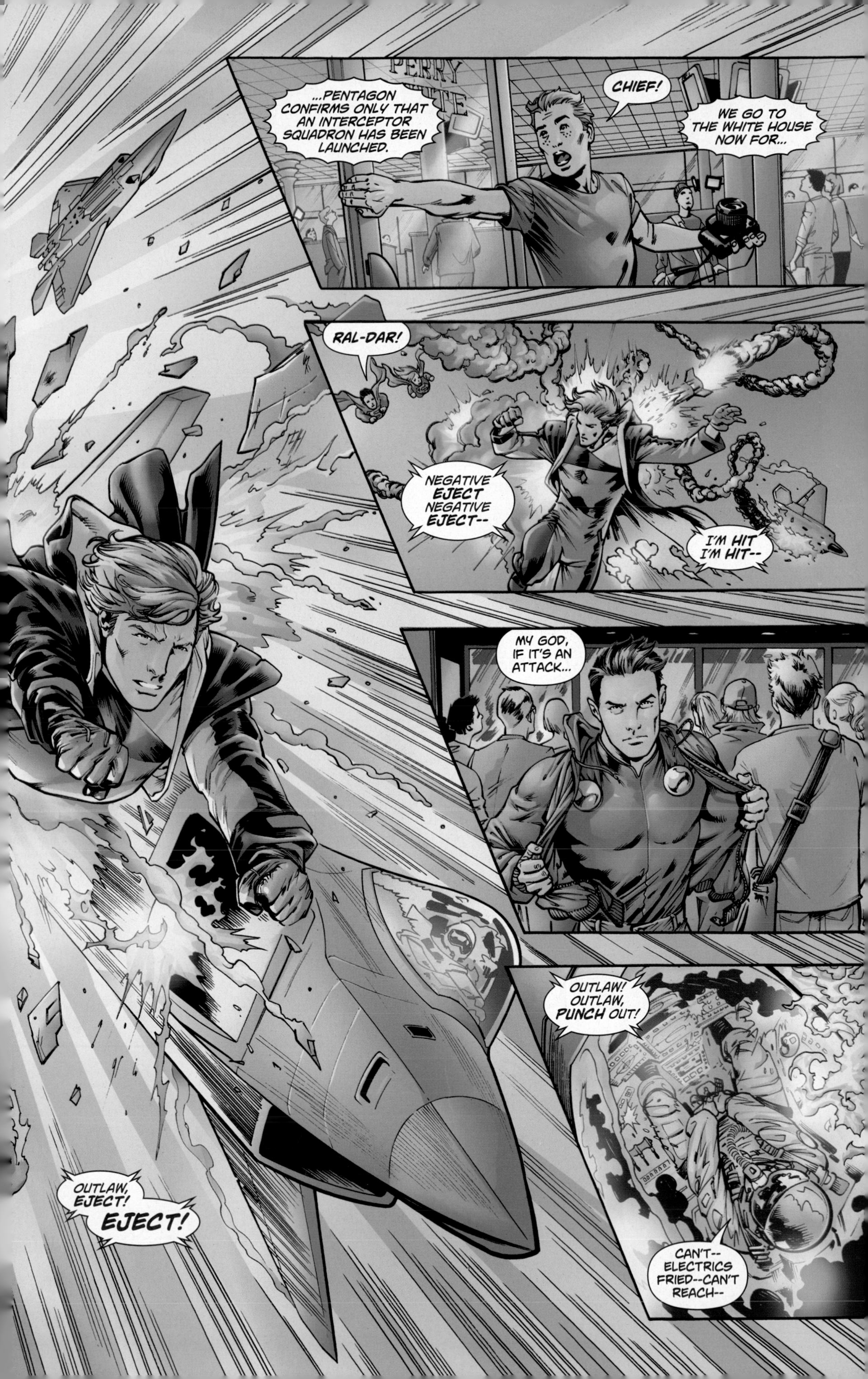
PERRY
...PENTAGON CONFIRMS ONLY THAT AN INTERCEPTOR SQUADRON HAS BEEN LAUNCHED.
CHIEF!
WE GO TO THE WHITE HOUSE NOW FOR...
RAL-DAR!
NEGATIVE EJECT NEGATIVE EJECT--
I'M HIT I'M HIT--
MY GOD, IF IT'S AN ATTACK...
OUTLAW! OUTLAW, PUNCH OUT!
CAN'T-- ELECTRICS FRIED--CAN'T REACH--
OUTLAW, EJECT! EJECT!

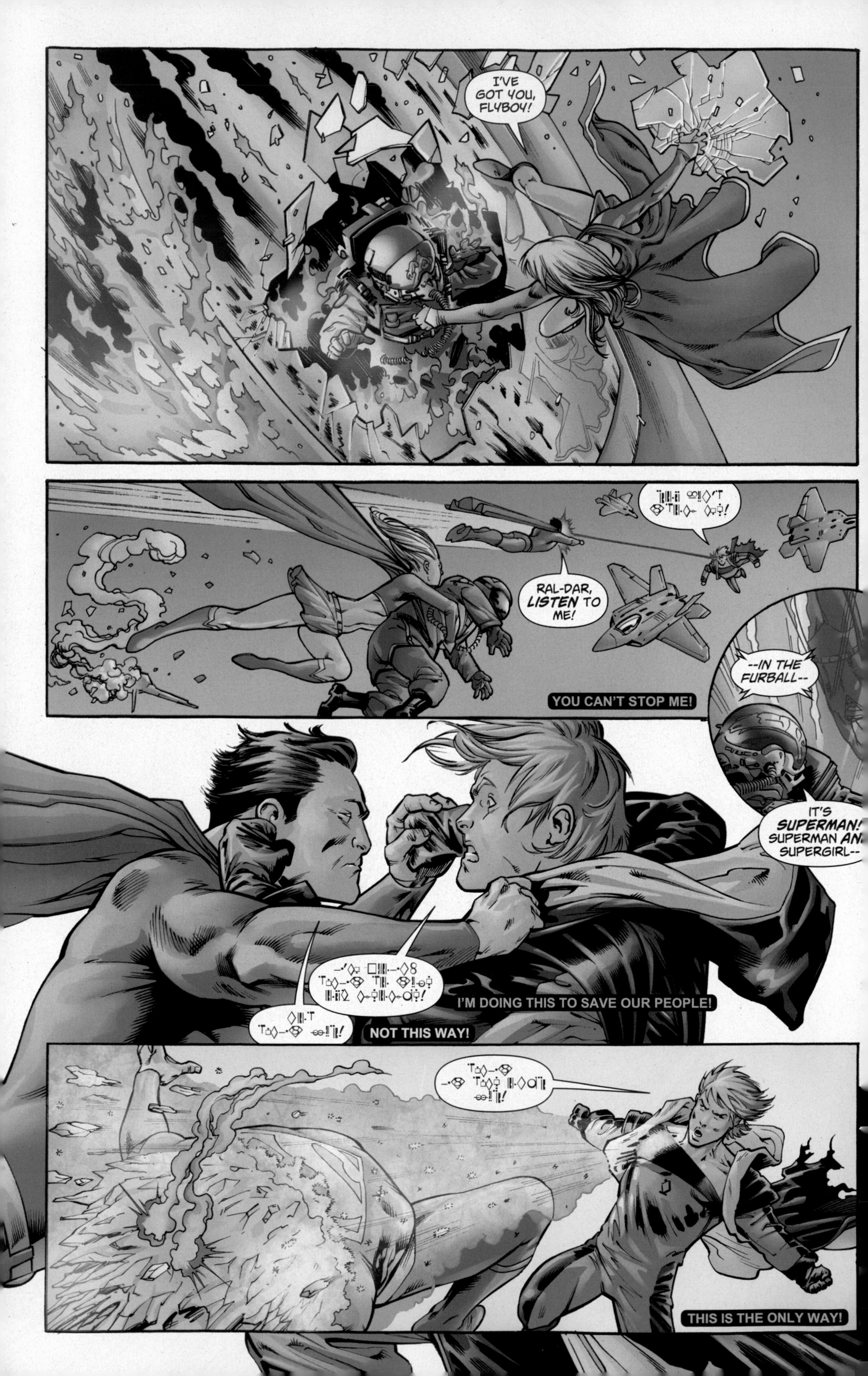
I'VE GOT YOU, FLYBOY!
RAL-DAR, LISTEN TO ME!
YOU CAN'T STOP ME!
--IN THE FURBALL--
IT'S SUPERMAN! SUPERMAN AN SUPERGIRL--
I'M DOING THIS TO SAVE OUR PEOPLE!
NOT THIS WAY!
THIS IS THE ONLY WAY!

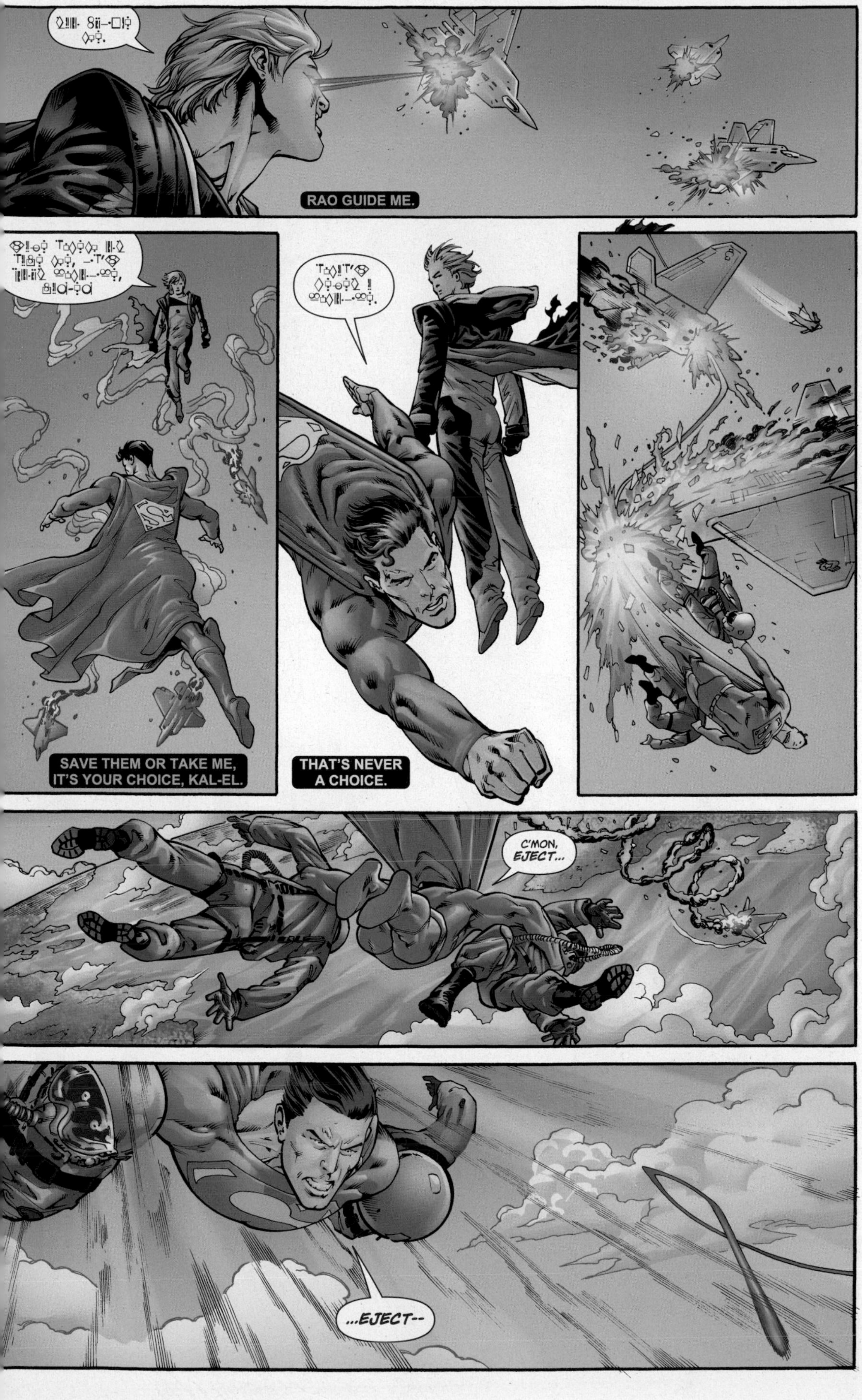

RAO GUIDE ME.
SAVE THEM OR TAKE ME, IT'S YOUR CHOICE, KAL-EL.
THAT'S NEVER A CHOICE.
C'MON, EJECT...
...EJECT--

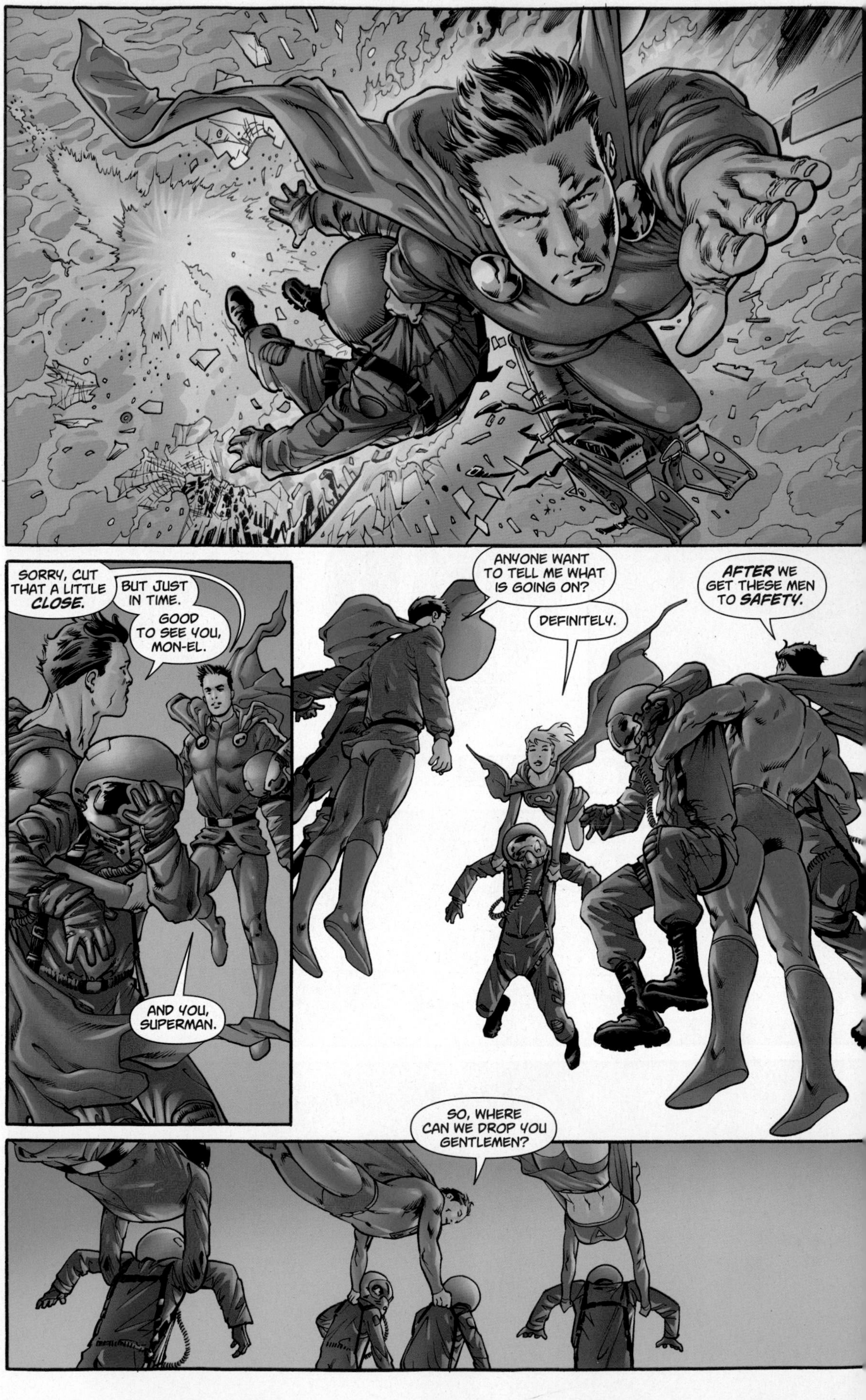
SORRY, CUT THAT A LITTLE **CLOSE.**
BUT JUST IN TIME.
GOOD TO SEE YOU, MON-EL.
AND YOU, SUPERMAN.
ANYONE WANT TO TELL ME WHAT IS GOING ON?
DEFINITELY.
AFTER WE GET THESE MEN TO **SAFETY.**
SO, WHERE CAN WE DROP YOU GENTLEMEN?

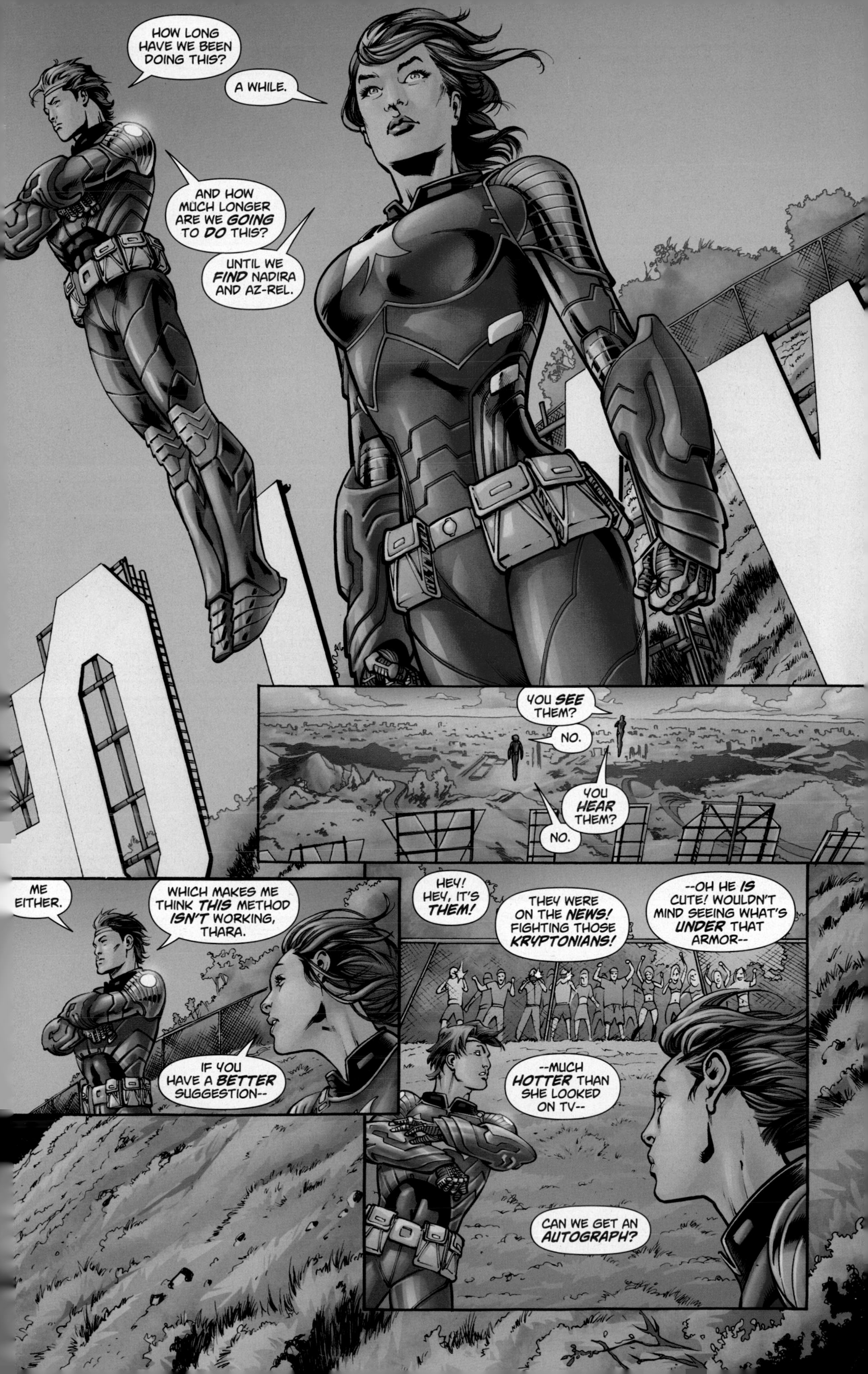
HOW LONG HAVE WE BEEN DOING THIS?
A WHILE.
AND HOW MUCH LONGER ARE WE GOING TO DO THIS?
UNTIL WE FIND NADIRA AND AZ-REL.
YOU SEE THEM?
NO.
YOU HEAR THEM?
NO.
ME EITHER.
WHICH MAKES ME THINK THIS METHOD ISN'T WORKING, THARA.
IF YOU HAVE A BETTER SUGGESTION--
HEY! HEY, IT'S THEM!
THEY WERE ON THE NEWS! FIGHTING THOSE KRYPTONIANS!
--OH HE IS CUTE! WOULDN'T MIND SEEING WHAT'S UNDER THAT ARMOR--
--MUCH HOTTER THAN SHE LOOKED ON TV--
CAN WE GET AN AUTOGRAPH?

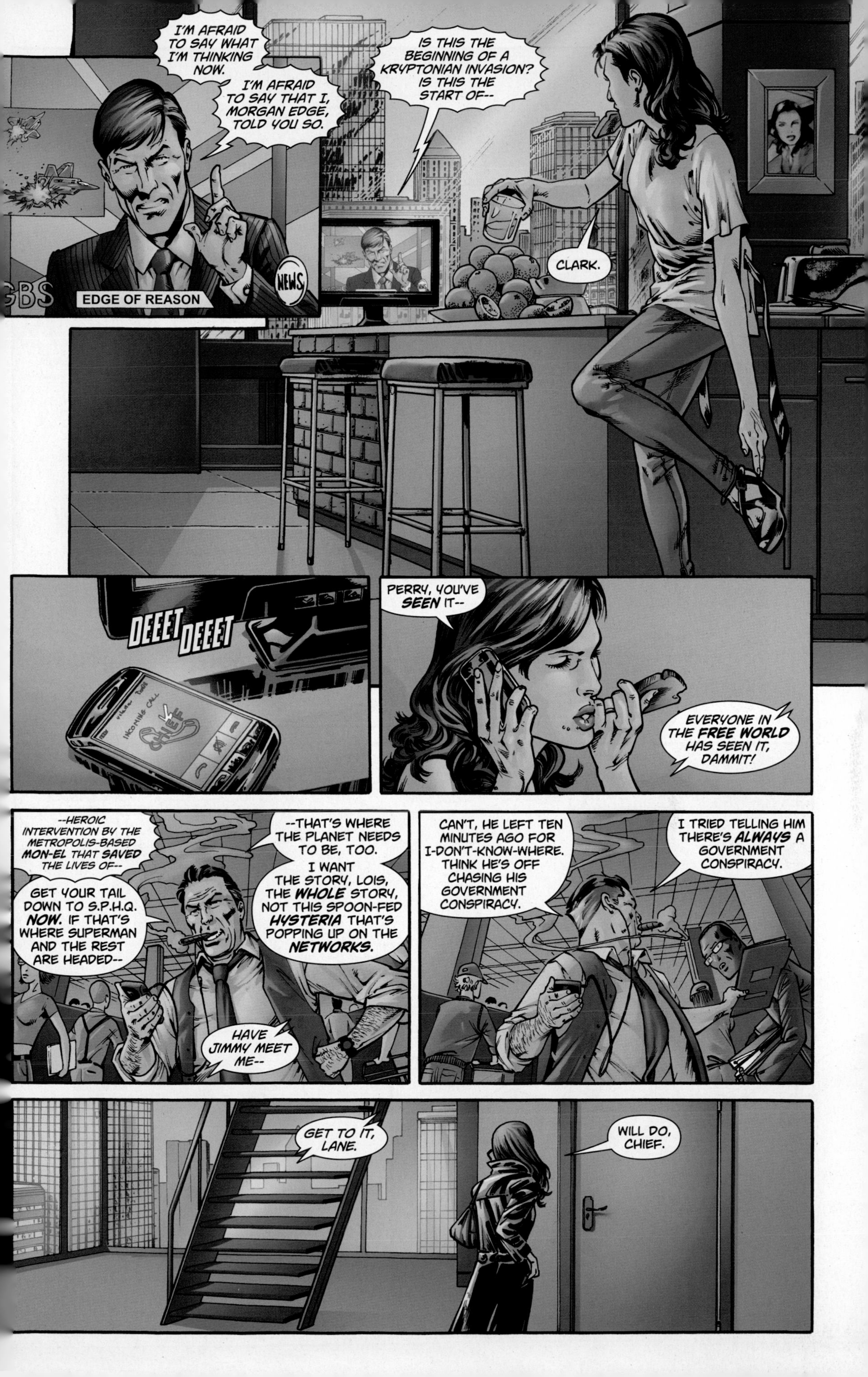
I'M AFRAID TO SAY WHAT I'M THINKING NOW.
I'M AFRAID TO SAY THAT I, MORGAN EDGE, TOLD YOU SO.
GBS
EDGE OF REASON
NEWS
IS THIS THE BEGINNING OF A KRYPTONIAN INVASION? IS THIS THE START OF--
CLARK.
DEEET DEEET
INCOMING CALL
CHIEF
PERRY, YOU'VE SEEN IT--
EVERYONE IN THE FREE WORLD HAS SEEN IT, DAMMIT!
--HEROIC INTERVENTION BY THE METROPOLIS-BASED MON-EL THAT SAVED THE LIVES OF--
GET YOUR TAIL DOWN TO S.P.H.Q. NOW. IF THAT'S WHERE SUPERMAN AND THE REST ARE HEADED--
--THAT'S WHERE THE PLANET NEEDS TO BE, TOO.
I WANT THE STORY, LOIS, THE WHOLE STORY, NOT THIS SPOON-FED HYSTERIA THAT'S POPPING UP ON THE NETWORKS.
HAVE JIMMY MEET ME--
CAN'T, HE LEFT TEN MINUTES AGO FOR I-DON'T-KNOW-WHERE. THINK HE'S OFF CHASING HIS GOVERNMENT CONSPIRACY.
I TRIED TELLING HIM THERE'S ALWAYS A GOVERNMENT CONSPIRACY.
GET TO IT, LANE.
WILL DO, CHIEF.

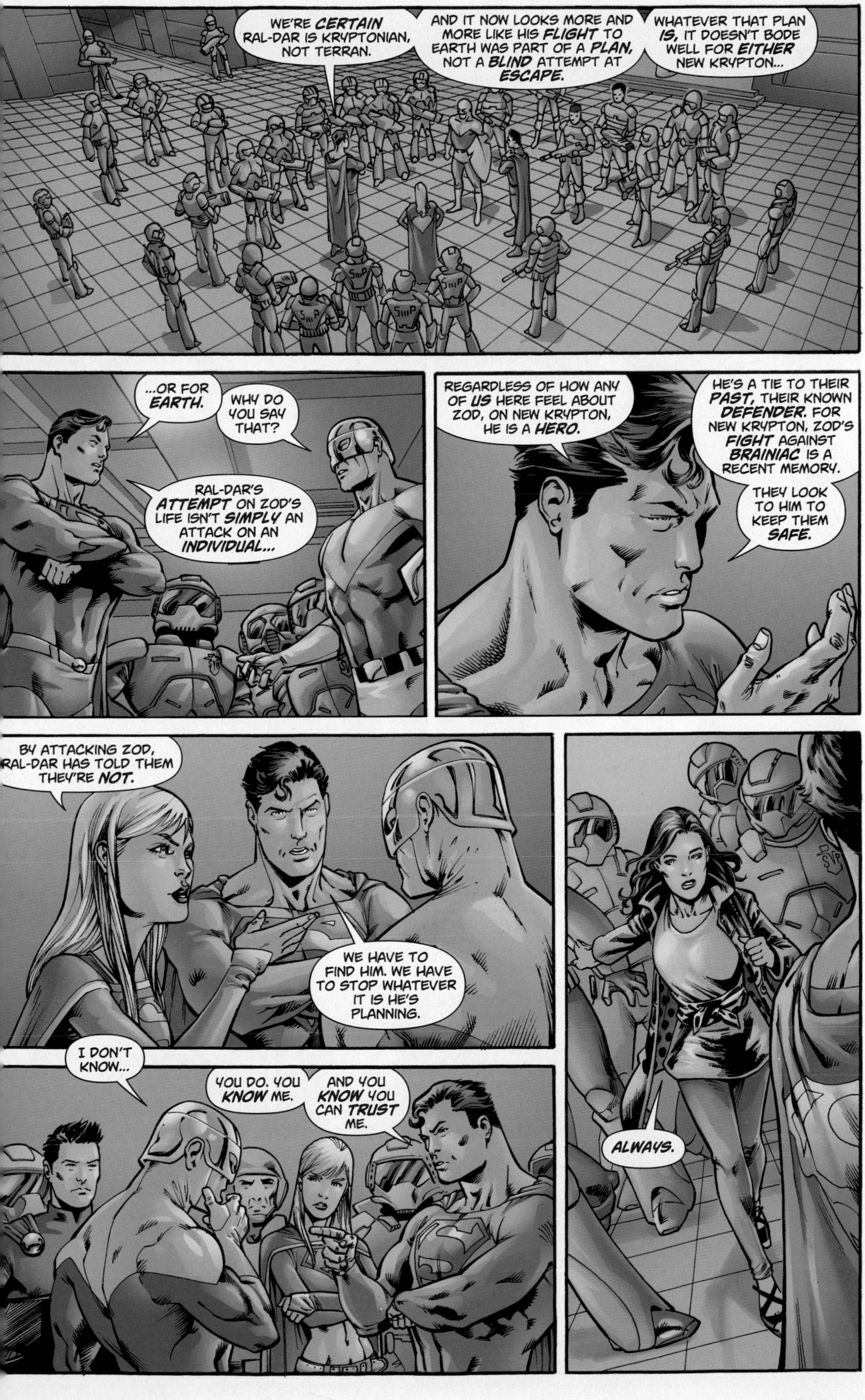

WE'RE CERTAIN RAL-DAR IS KRYPTONIAN, NOT TERRAN.
AND IT NOW LOOKS MORE AND MORE LIKE HIS FLIGHT TO EARTH WAS PART OF A PLAN, NOT A BLIND ATTEMPT AT ESCAPE.
WHATEVER THAT PLAN IS, IT DOESN'T BODE WELL FOR EITHER NEW KRYPTON...
...OR FOR EARTH.
WHY DO YOU SAY THAT?
RAL-DAR'S ATTEMPT ON ZOD'S LIFE ISN'T SIMPLY AN ATTACK ON AN INDIVIDUAL...
REGARDLESS OF HOW ANY OF US HERE FEEL ABOUT ZOD, ON NEW KRYPTON, HE IS A HERO.
HE'S A TIE TO THEIR PAST, THEIR KNOWN DEFENDER. FOR NEW KRYPTON, ZOD'S FIGHT AGAINST BRAINIAC IS A RECENT MEMORY.
THEY LOOK TO HIM TO KEEP THEM SAFE.
BY ATTACKING ZOD, RAL-DAR HAS TOLD THEM THEY'RE NOT.
WE HAVE TO FIND HIM. WE HAVE TO STOP WHATEVER IT IS HE'S PLANNING.
I DON'T KNOW...
YOU DO. YOU KNOW ME.
AND YOU KNOW YOU CAN TRUST ME.
ALWAYS.

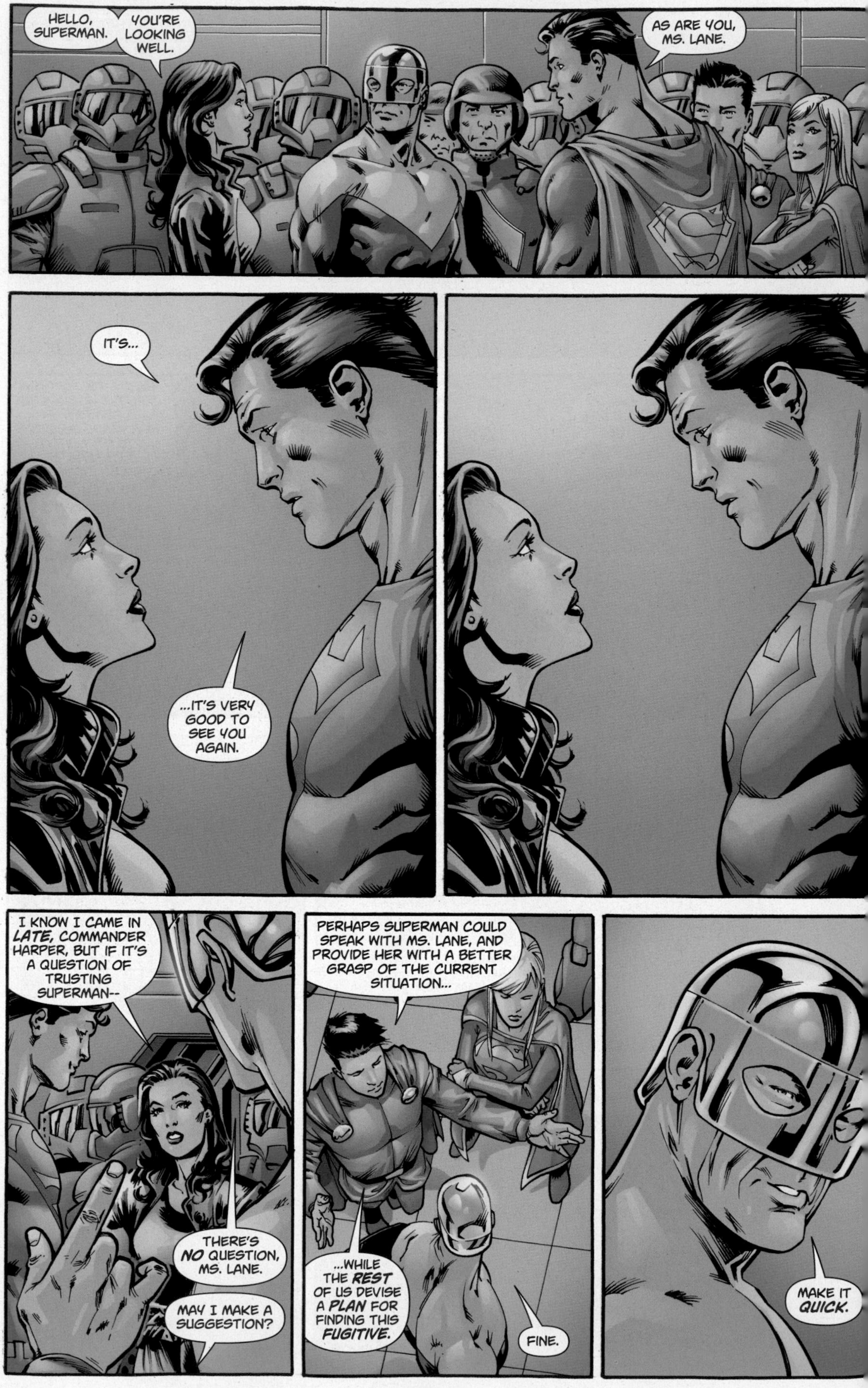
HELLO, SUPERMAN.
YOU'RE LOOKING WELL.
AS ARE YOU, MS. LANE.
IT'S...
...IT'S VERY GOOD TO SEE YOU AGAIN.
I KNOW I CAME IN LATE, COMMANDER HARPER, BUT IF IT'S A QUESTION OF TRUSTING SUPERMAN--
THERE'S NO QUESTION, MS. LANE.
MAY I MAKE A SUGGESTION?
PERHAPS SUPERMAN COULD SPEAK WITH MS. LANE, AND PROVIDE HER WITH A BETTER GRASP OF THE CURRENT SITUATION...
...WHILE THE REST OF US DEVISE A PLAN FOR FINDING THIS FUGITIVE.
FINE.
MAKE IT QUICK.

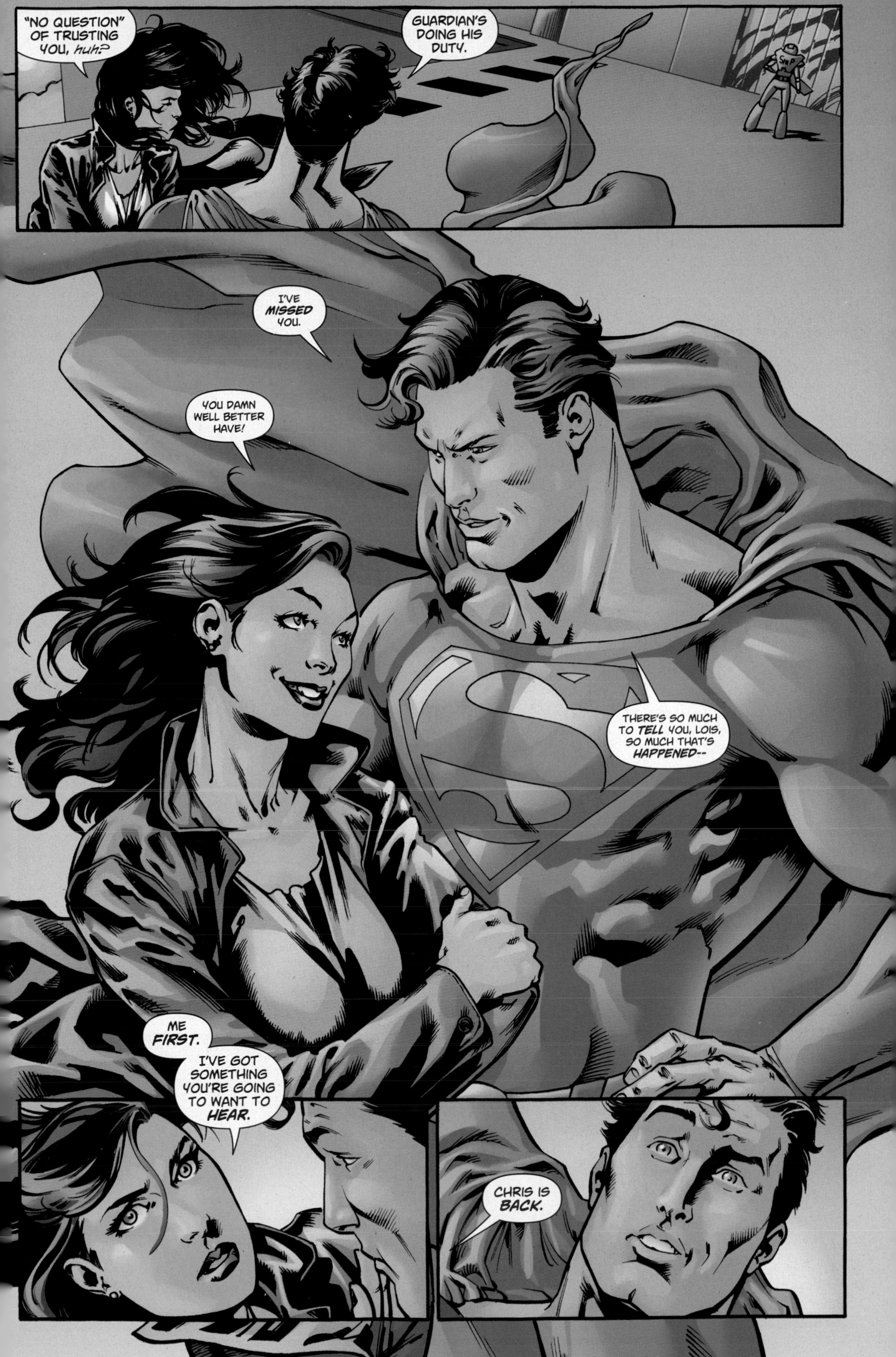
"NO QUESTION" OF TRUSTING YOU, *huh?*
GUARDIAN'S DOING HIS DUTY.
I'VE **MISSED** YOU.
YOU DAMN WELL BETTER HAVE!
THERE'S SO MUCH TO **TELL** YOU, LOIS, SO MUCH THAT'S **HAPPENED**--
ME **FIRST**.
I'VE GOT SOMETHING YOU'RE GOING TO WANT TO **HEAR**.
CHRIS IS **BACK**.

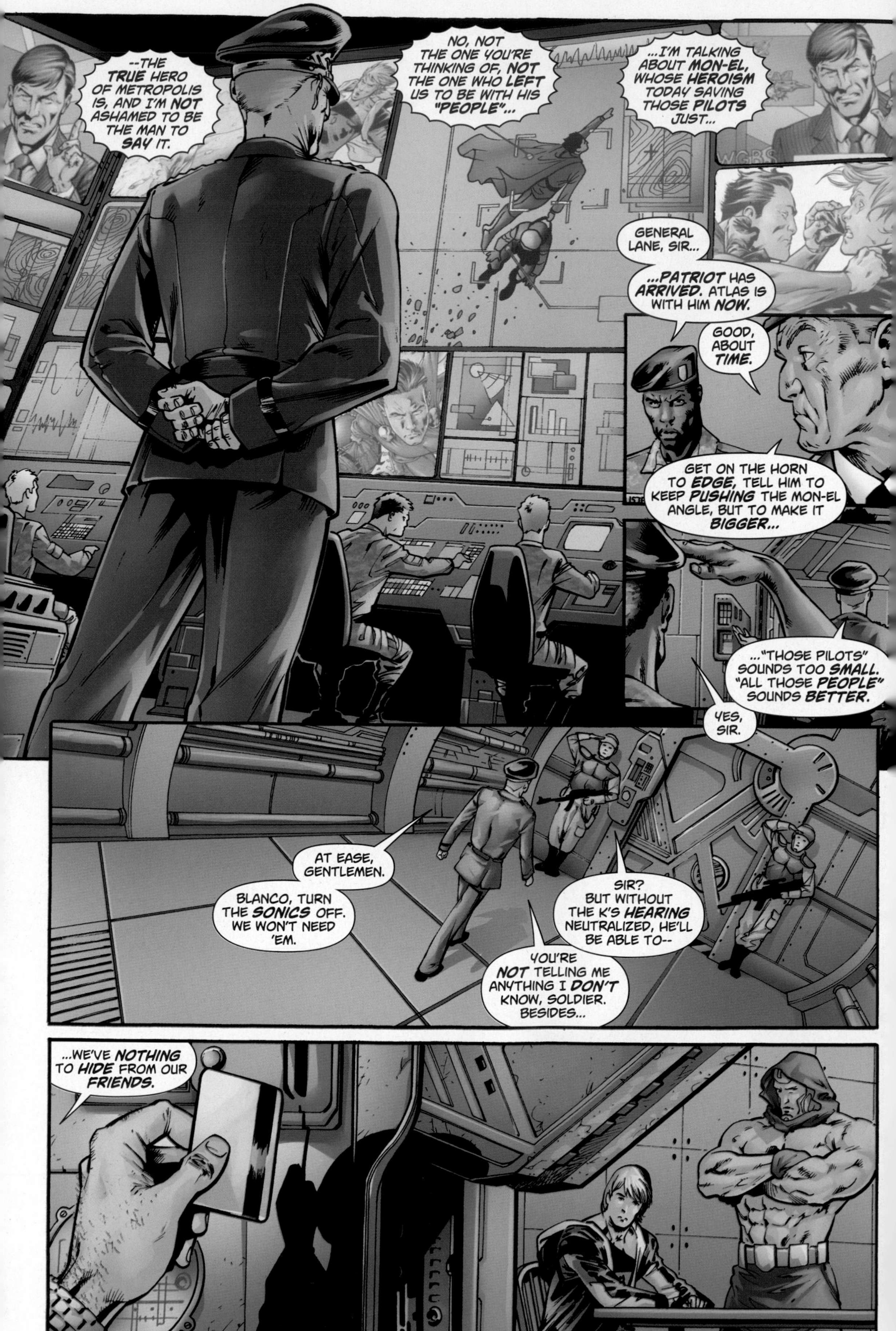
--THE TRUE HERO OF METROPOLIS IS, AND I'M NOT ASHAMED TO BE THE MAN TO SAY IT.
NO, NOT THE ONE YOU'RE THINKING OF, NOT THE ONE WHO LEFT US TO BE WITH HIS "PEOPLE"...
...I'M TALKING ABOUT MON-EL, WHOSE HEROISM TODAY SAVING THOSE PILOTS JUST...
WGBS
GENERAL LANE, SIR...
...PATRIOT HAS ARRIVED. ATLAS IS WITH HIM NOW.
GOOD, ABOUT TIME.
GET ON THE HORN TO EDGE, TELL HIM TO KEEP PUSHING THE MON-EL ANGLE, BUT TO MAKE IT BIGGER...
..."THOSE PILOTS" SOUNDS TOO SMALL. "ALL THOSE PEOPLE" SOUNDS BETTER.
YES, SIR.
AT EASE, GENTLEMEN.
BLANCO, TURN THE SONICS OFF. WE WON'T NEED 'EM.
SIR? BUT WITHOUT THE K'S HEARING NEUTRALIZED, HE'LL BE ABLE TO--
YOU'RE NOT TELLING ME ANYTHING I DON'T KNOW, SOLDIER. BESIDES...
...WE'VE NOTHING TO HIDE FROM OUR FRIENDS.

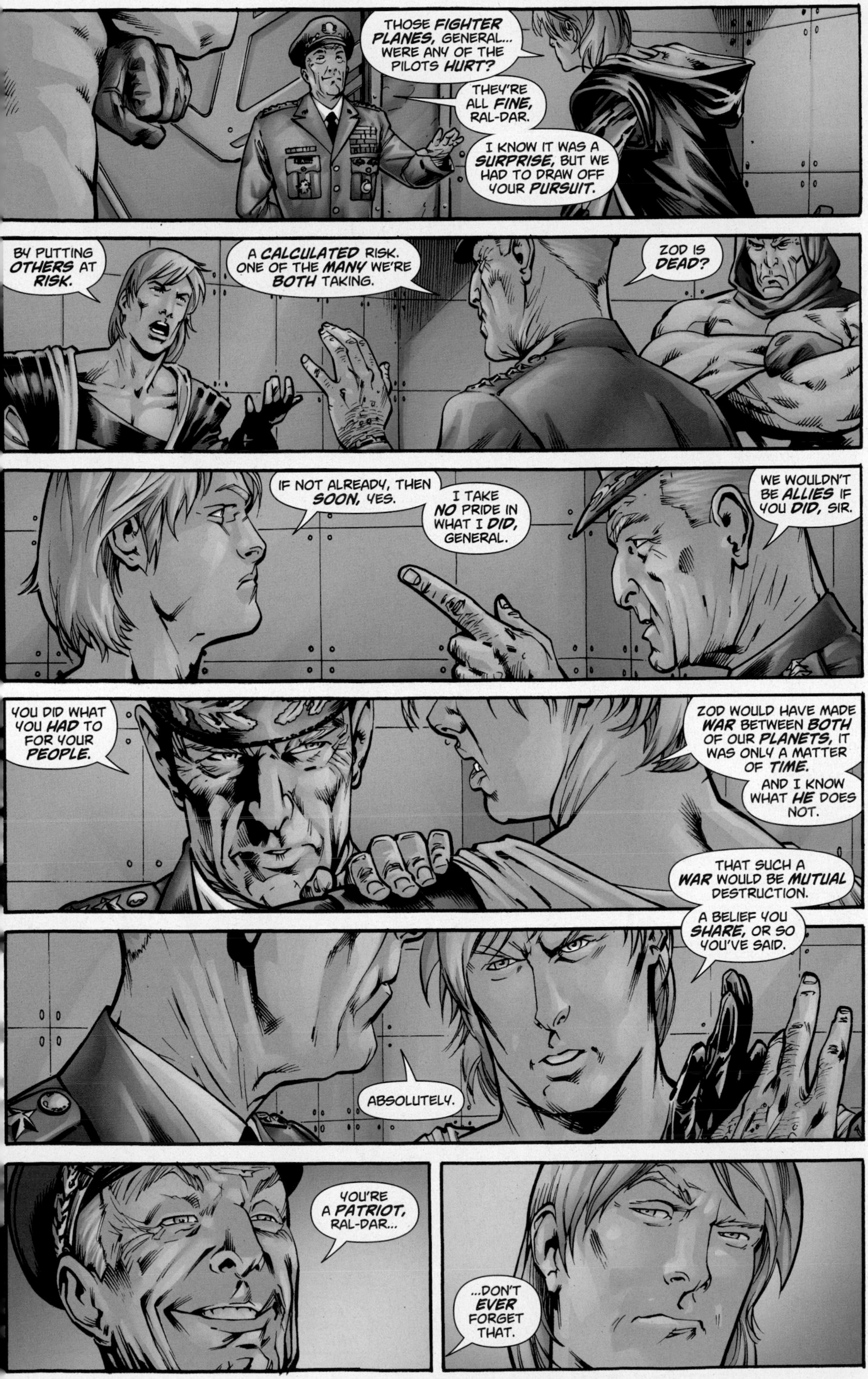
THOSE FIGHTER PLANES, GENERAL... WERE ANY OF THE PILOTS HURT?
THEY'RE ALL FINE, RAL-DAR.
I KNOW IT WAS A SURPRISE, BUT WE HAD TO DRAW OFF YOUR PURSUIT.
BY PUTTING OTHERS AT RISK.
A CALCULATED RISK. ONE OF THE MANY WE'RE BOTH TAKING.
ZOD IS DEAD?
IF NOT ALREADY, THEN SOON, YES.
I TAKE NO PRIDE IN WHAT I DID, GENERAL.
WE WOULDN'T BE ALLIES IF YOU DID, SIR.
YOU DID WHAT YOU HAD TO FOR YOUR PEOPLE.
ZOD WOULD HAVE MADE WAR BETWEEN BOTH OF OUR PLANETS, IT WAS ONLY A MATTER OF TIME.
AND I KNOW WHAT HE DOES NOT.
THAT SUCH A WAR WOULD BE MUTUAL DESTRUCTION.
A BELIEF YOU SHARE, OR SO YOU'VE SAID.
ABSOLUTELY.
YOU'RE A PATRIOT, RAL-DAR...
...DON'T EVER FORGET THAT.

--FILMING A MOVIE MAYBE--

--THEM! ON THE NEWS, YOU SEE--

--MARKOVIA, WHILE COMMENTING ON THE RECENT KRYPTONIAN INCURSION--

--BACKING UP ON THE HOLLYWOOD FREEWAY AND THE--

--SPOTTED IN METROPOLIS, WHERE SUPERMAN, SUPERGIRL, AND MON-EL ARE MEETING WITH THE SCIENCE POLICE--

WAIT!

YOU *FOUND* THEM?

NO, NO, *LISTEN...*

...IT'S ON THE *NEWS,* THEY'RE TALKING ABOUT *SUPERMAN..*

HE'S COME *BACK!* SUPERGIRL, TOO! THEY'RE IN *METROPOLIS!*

WE COULD BE THERE IN A *COUPLE* OF MINUTES, THARA!

WE HAVE TO *FIND* NADIRA AND AZ-REL *FIRST.*

BUT HE COULD *HELP* US! SUPERGIRL, TOO!

I *DON'T* WANT SUPERGIRL'S *HELP.*

FINE, SUPERMAN'S THEN!

YOU'RE NOT *THINKING!* THESE *PEOPLE,* THESE *HUMANS,* THEY THINK WE'RE ONE OF *THEM!*

IF WE *TEAM UP* WITH SUPERMAN, WE *LOSE* THAT, WE'LL BLOW OUR *COVER!*

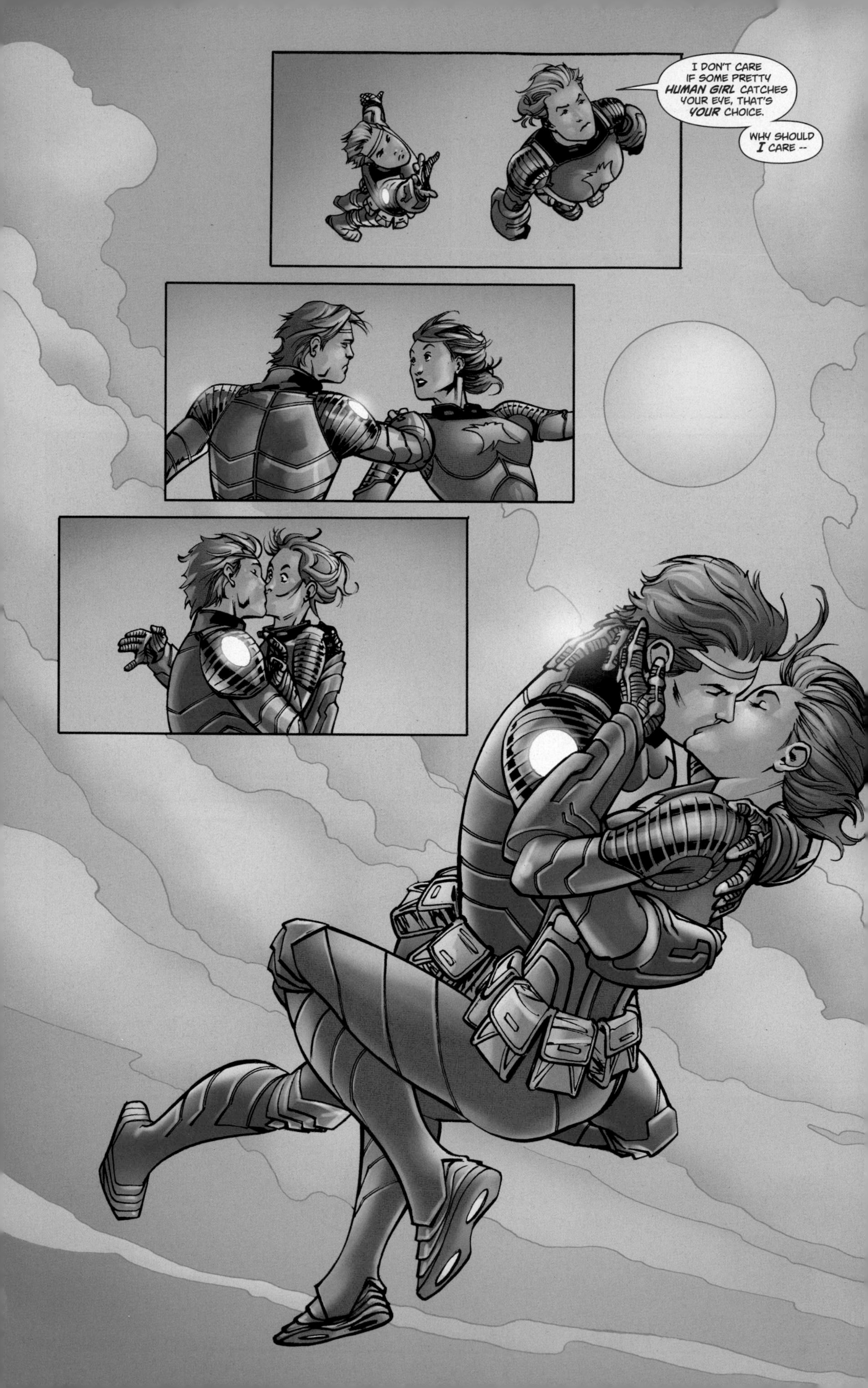
I DON'T CARE IF SOME PRETTY HUMAN GIRL CATCHES YOUR EYE, THAT'S YOUR CHOICE.
WHY SHOULD I CARE --

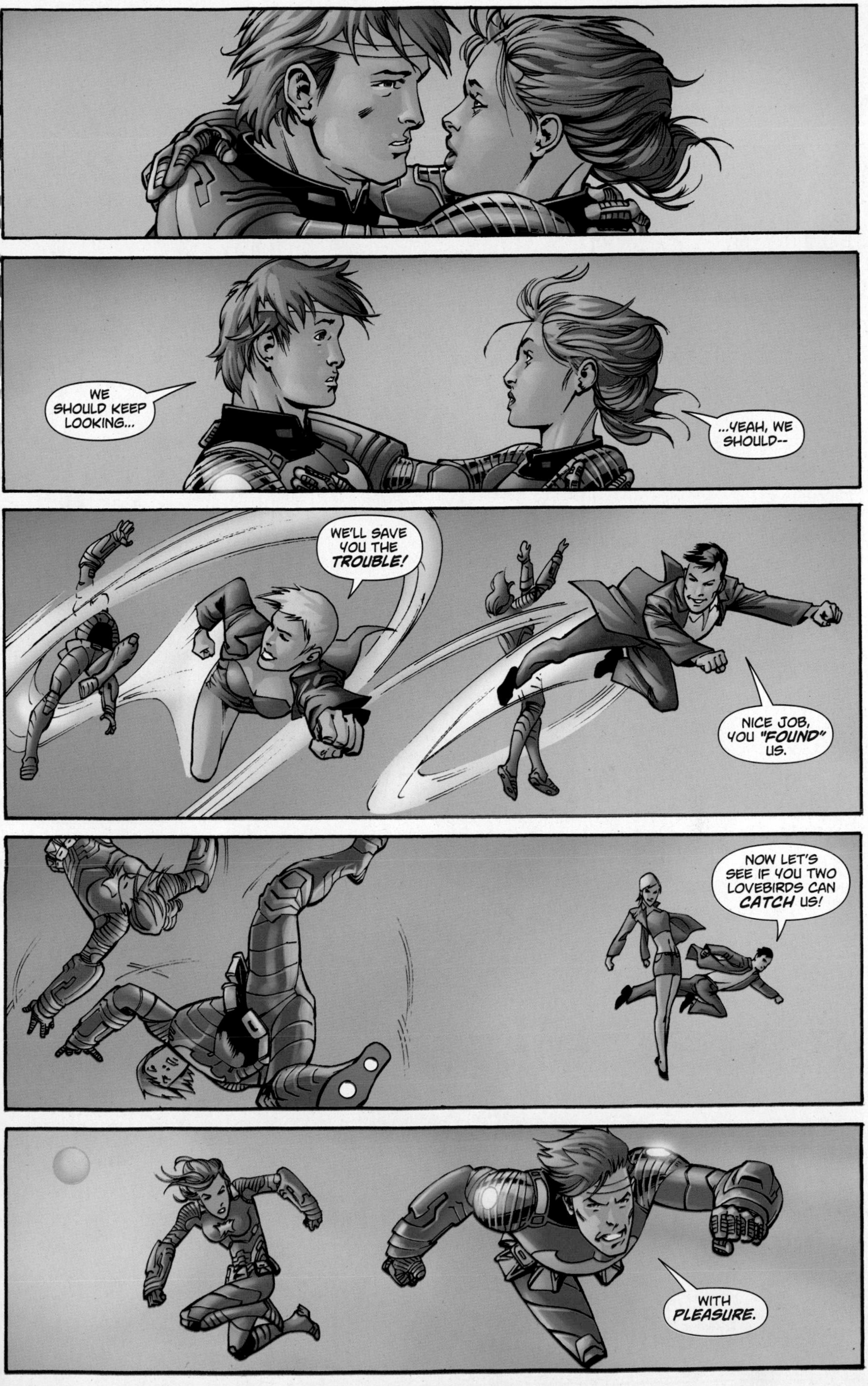
WE SHOULD KEEP LOOKING...
...YEAH, WE SHOULD--
WE'LL SAVE YOU THE TROUBLE!
NICE JOB, YOU "FOUND" US.
NOW LET'S SEE IF YOU TWO LOVEBIRDS CAN CATCH US!
WITH PLEASURE.

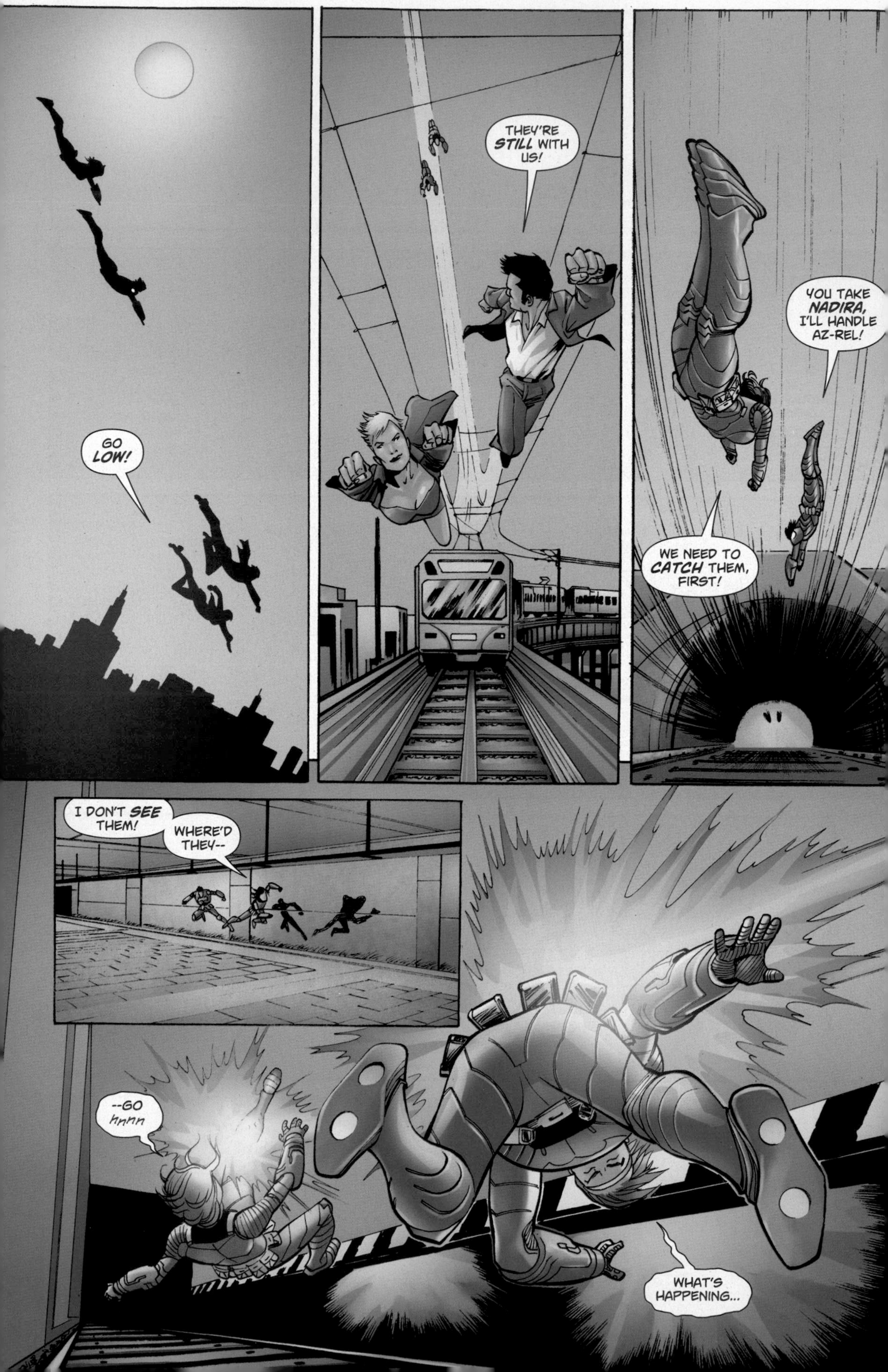
GO
LOW!
THEY'RE
STILL WITH
US!
YOU TAKE
NADIRA,
I'LL HANDLE
AZ-REL!
WE NEED TO
CATCH THEM,
FIRST!
I DON'T SEE
THEM!
WHERE'D
THEY--
--GO
hnnn
WHAT'S
HAPPENING...

<SUPERGIRL 44>
COVER ART BY **FERNANDO DAGNINO** & **RAÚL FERNANDEZ** WITH **MAZI**

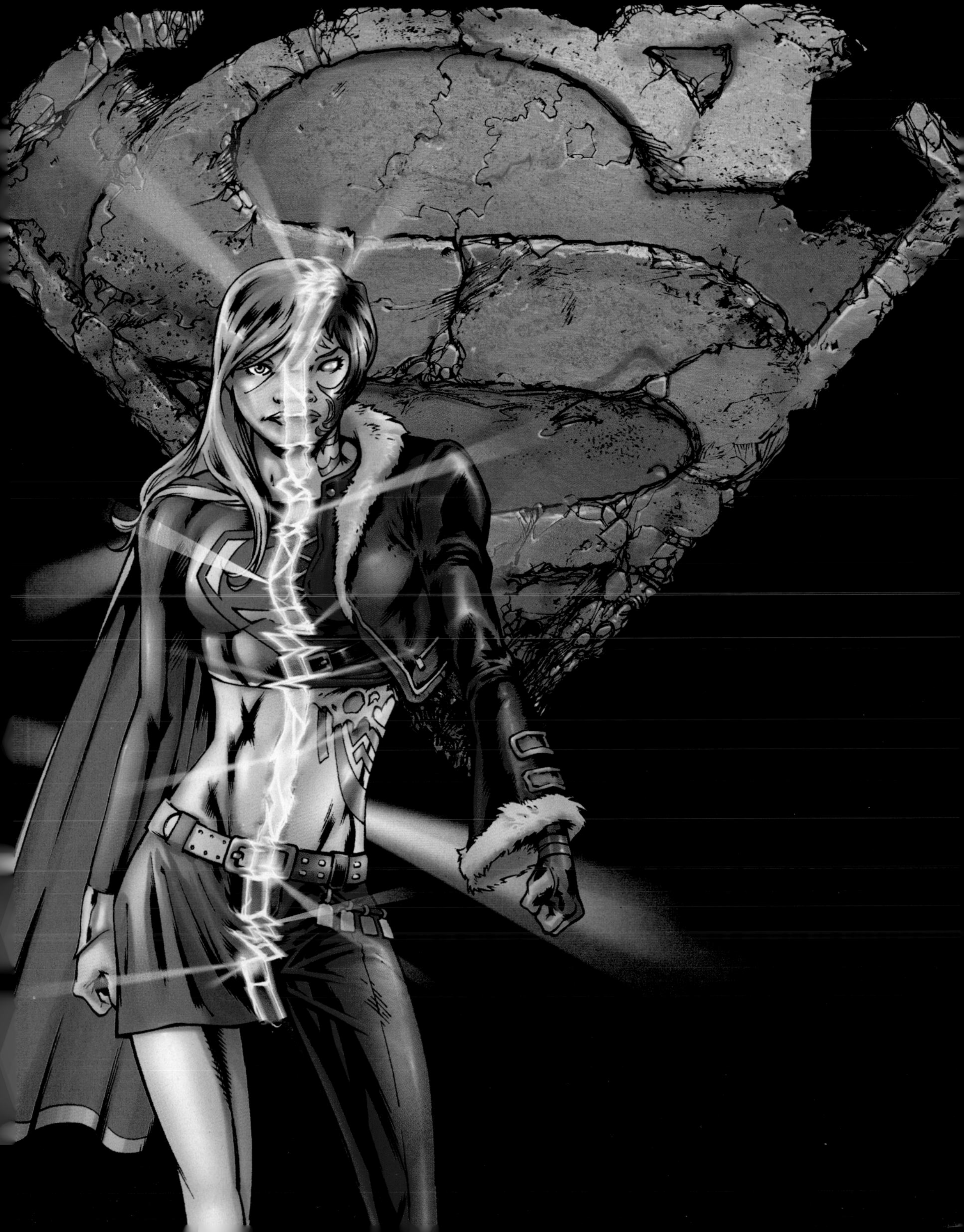

CODENAME: **PATRIOT** <PART THREE>
STERLING GATES - WRITER
JAMAL IGLE — PENCILLER
JON SIBAL — INKER

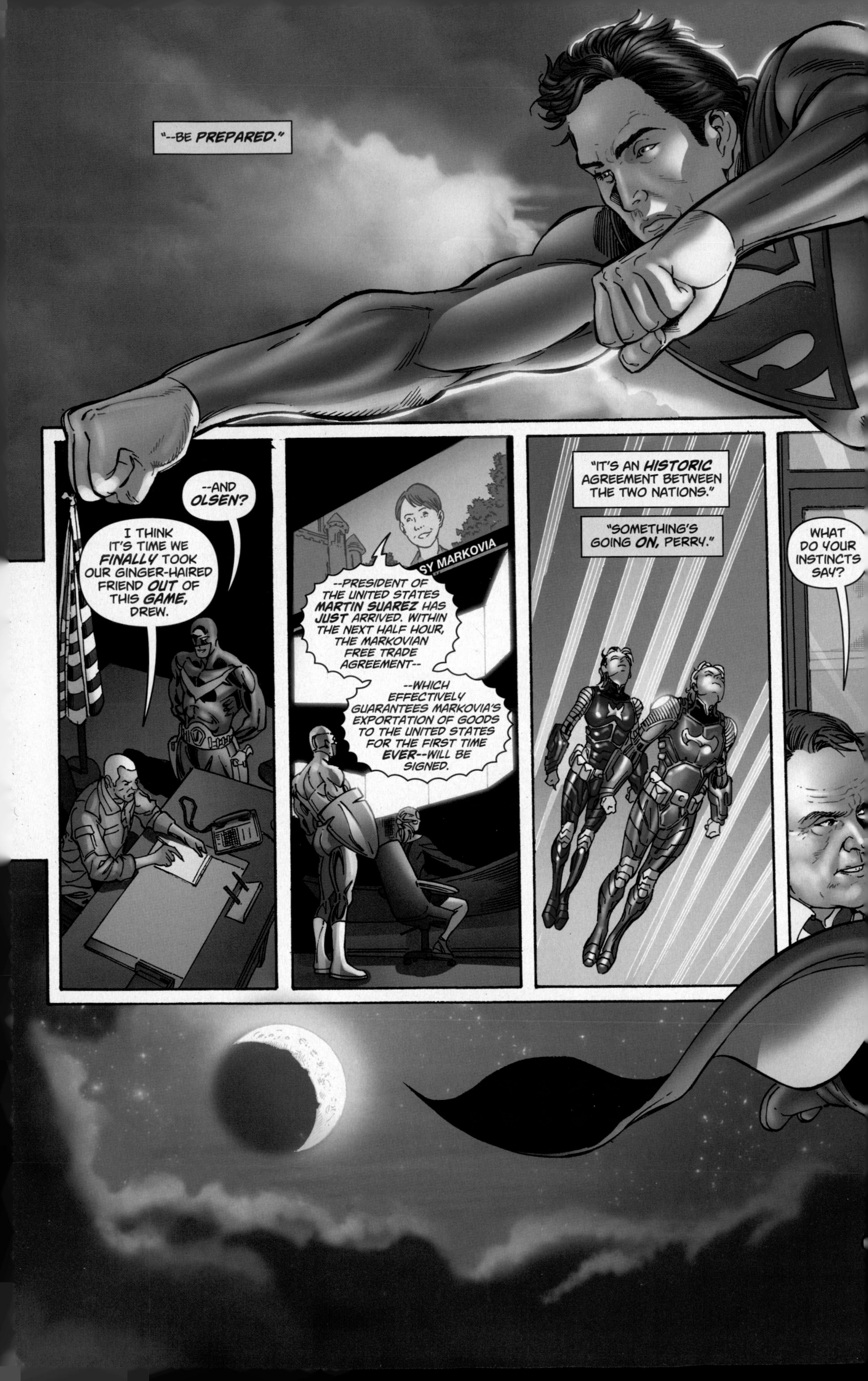
"--BE PREPARED."
--AND OLSEN?
I THINK IT'S TIME WE FINALLY TOOK OUR GINGER-HAIRED FRIEND OUT OF THIS GAME, DREW.
SY MARKOVIA
--PRESIDENT OF THE UNITED STATES MARTIN SUAREZ HAS JUST ARRIVED. WITHIN THE NEXT HALF HOUR, THE MARKOVIAN FREE TRADE AGREEMENT--
--WHICH EFFECTIVELY GUARANTEES MARKOVIA'S EXPORTATION OF GOODS TO THE UNITED STATES FOR THE FIRST TIME EVER--WILL BE SIGNED.
"IT'S AN HISTORIC AGREEMENT BETWEEN THE TWO NATIONS."
"SOMETHING'S GOING ON, PERRY."
WHAT DO YOUR INSTINCTS SAY?

COVER ART BY **FERNANDO DAGNINO** & **RAÚL FERNANDEZ** WITH **MAZI**

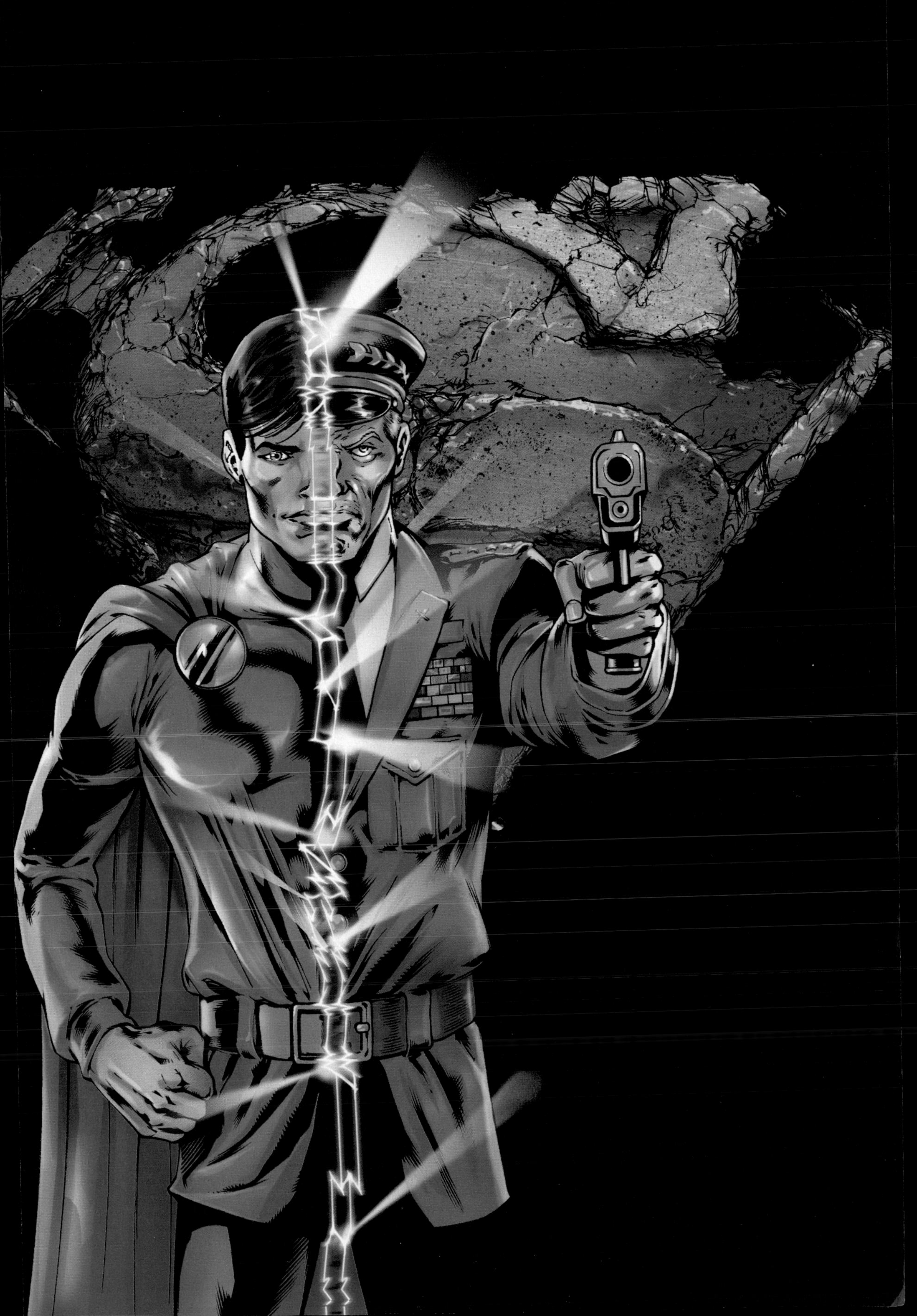

CODENAME: PATRIOT <PART FOUR>

JAMES ROBINSON – WRITER
RENATO GUEDES WITH EDUARDO PANSICA – PENCILLERS
JOSÉ WILSON MAGALHÃES WITH SANDRO RIBEIRO – INKERS

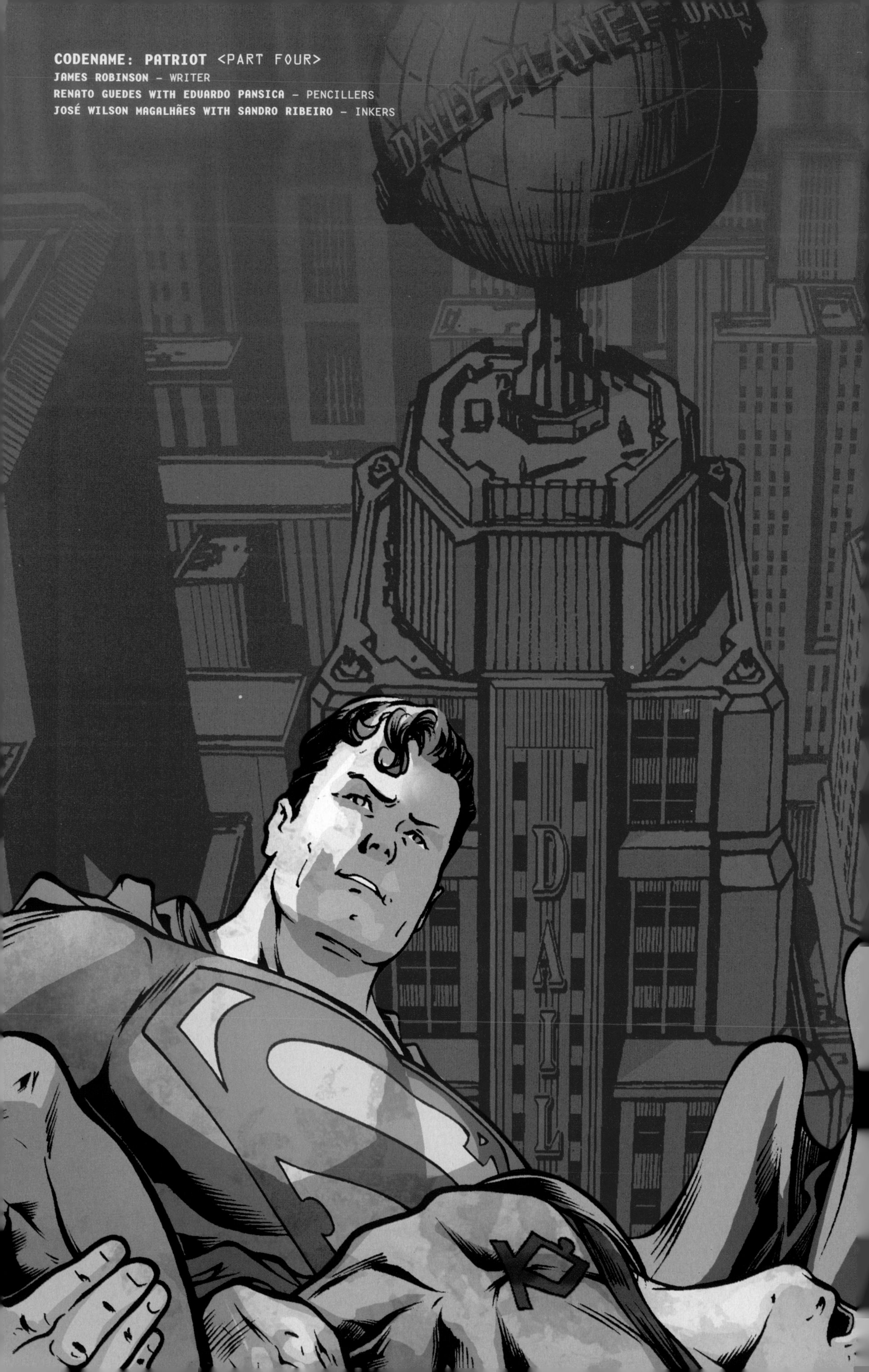
DAILY PLANET

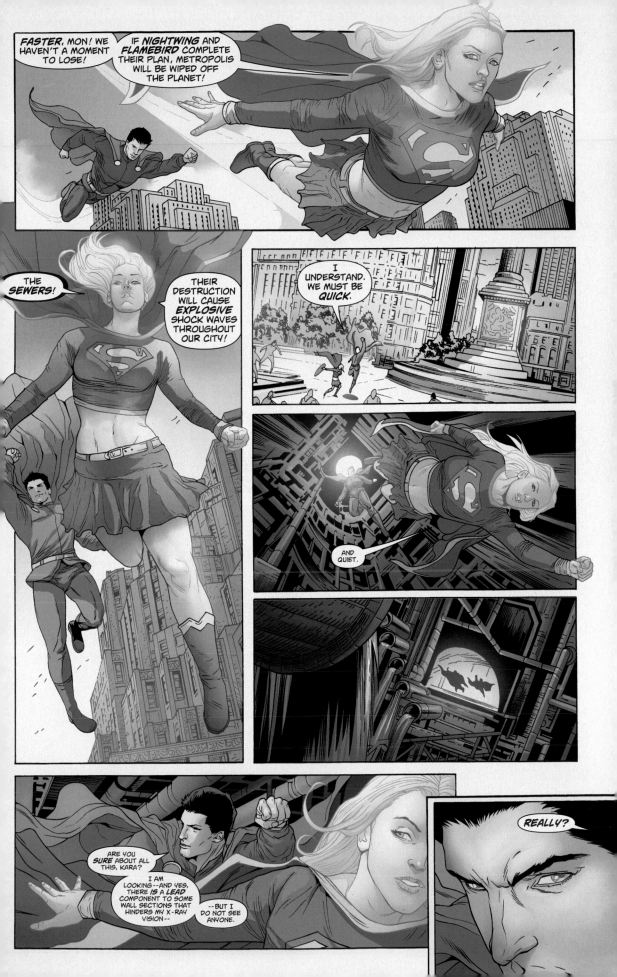

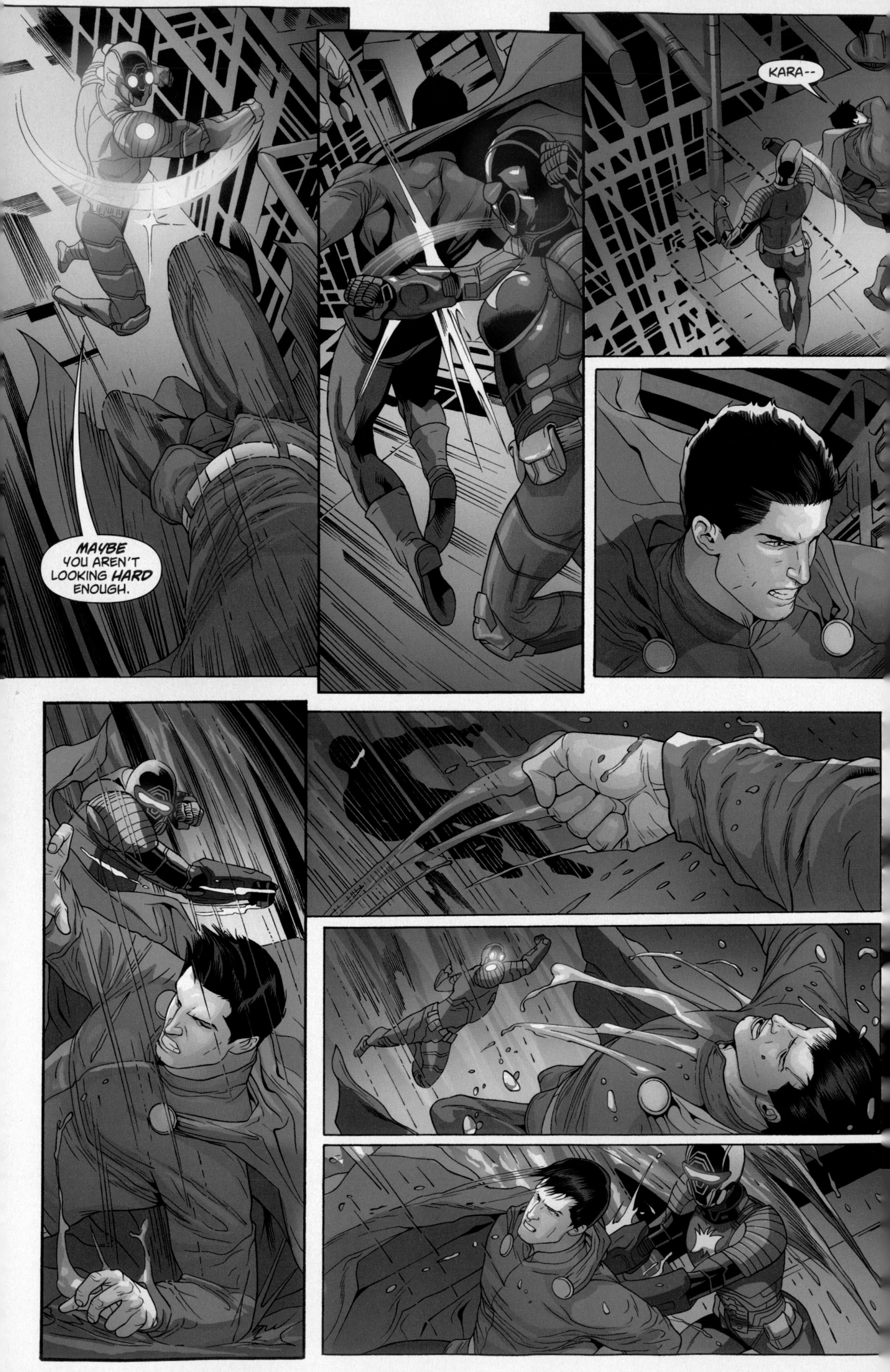
MAYBE YOU AREN'T LOOKING HARD ENOUGH.
KARA--

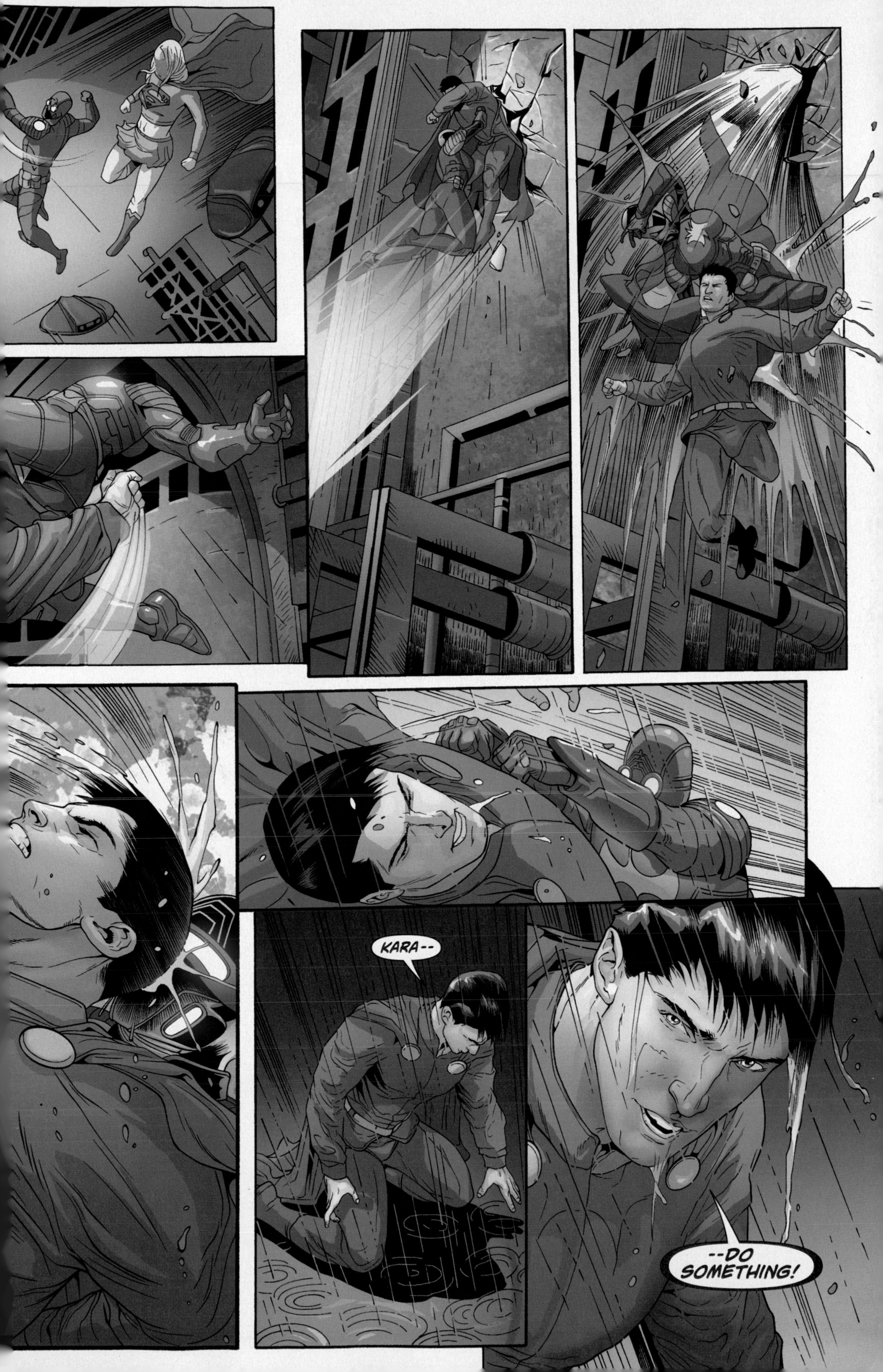
KARA--
--DO SOMETHING!

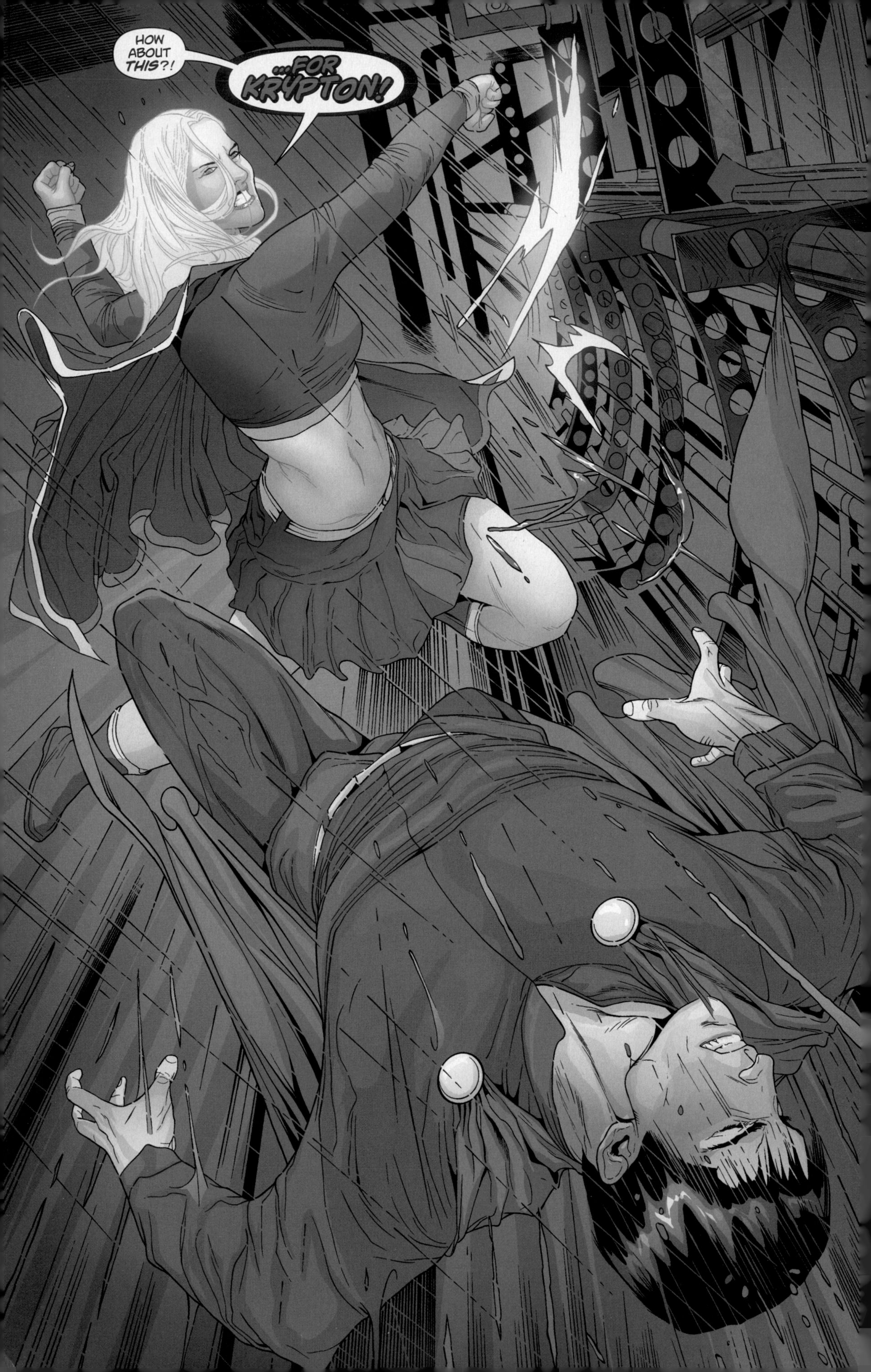
HOW ABOUT THIS?!
...FOR KRYPTON!

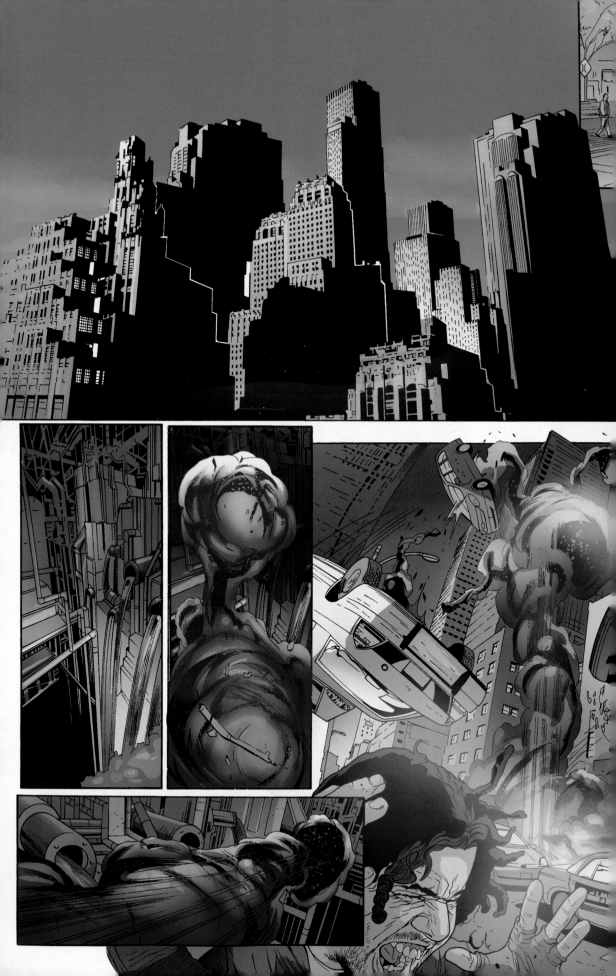

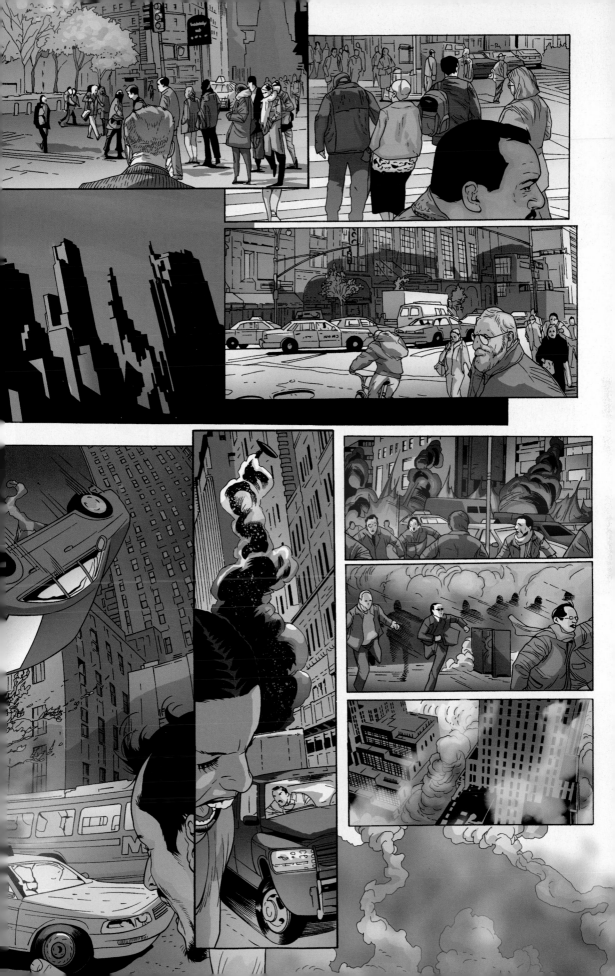

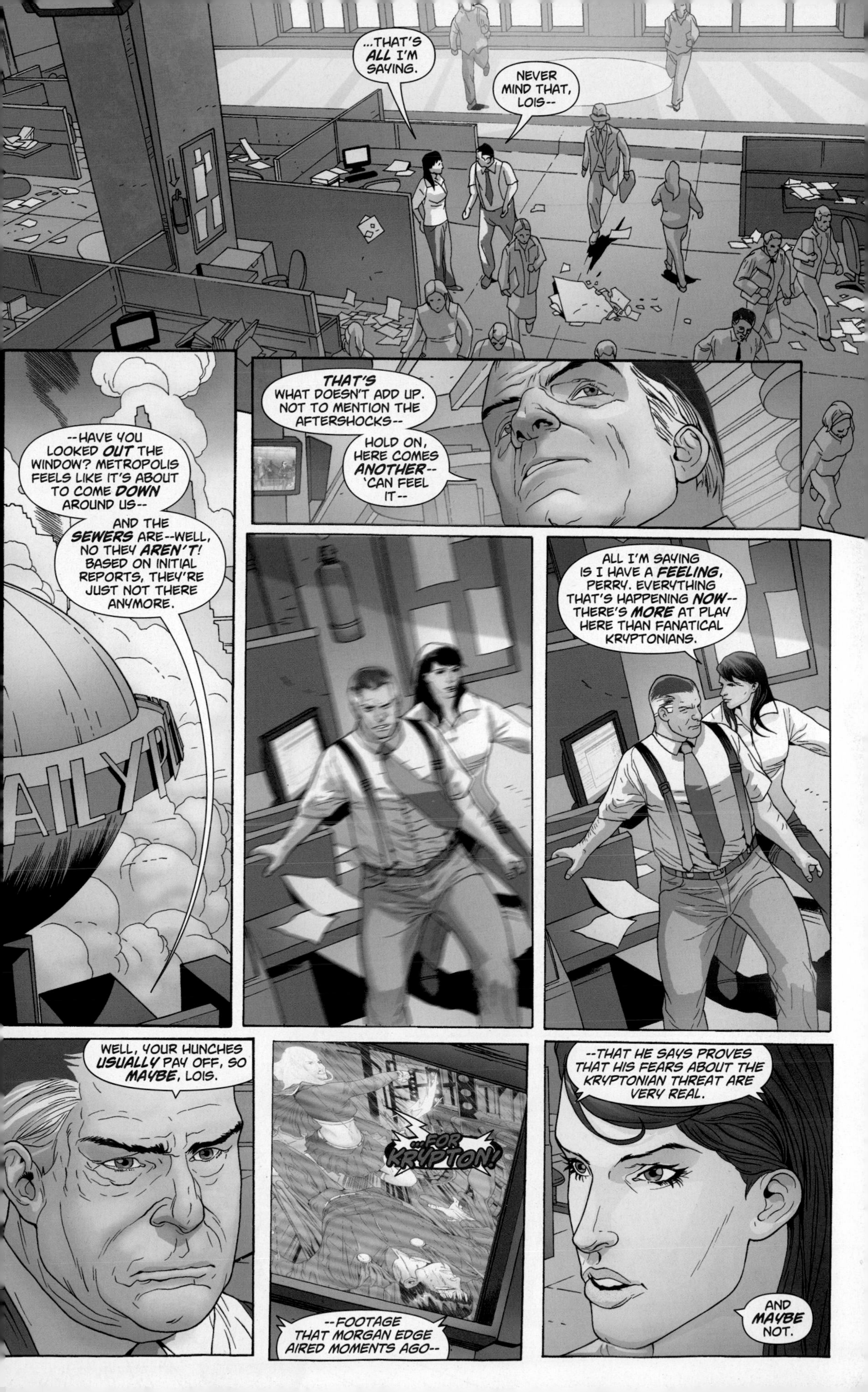
...THAT'S ALL I'M SAYING.
NEVER MIND THAT, LOIS--
--HAVE YOU LOOKED OUT THE WINDOW? METROPOLIS FEELS LIKE IT'S ABOUT TO COME DOWN AROUND US--
AND THE SEWERS ARE--WELL, NO THEY AREN'T! BASED ON INITIAL REPORTS, THEY'RE JUST NOT THERE ANYMORE.
AILY P
THAT'S WHAT DOESN'T ADD UP. NOT TO MENTION THE AFTERSHOCKS--
HOLD ON, HERE COMES ANOTHER-- 'CAN FEEL IT--
ALL I'M SAYING IS I HAVE A FEELING, PERRY. EVERYTHING THAT'S HAPPENING NOW-- THERE'S MORE AT PLAY HERE THAN FANATICAL KRYPTONIANS.
WELL, YOUR HUNCHES USUALLY PAY OFF, SO MAYBE, LOIS.
...FOR KRYPTON!
--FOOTAGE THAT MORGAN EDGE AIRED MOMENTS AGO--
--THAT HE SAYS PROVES THAT HIS FEARS ABOUT THE KRYPTONIAN THREAT ARE VERY REAL.
AND MAYBE NOT.

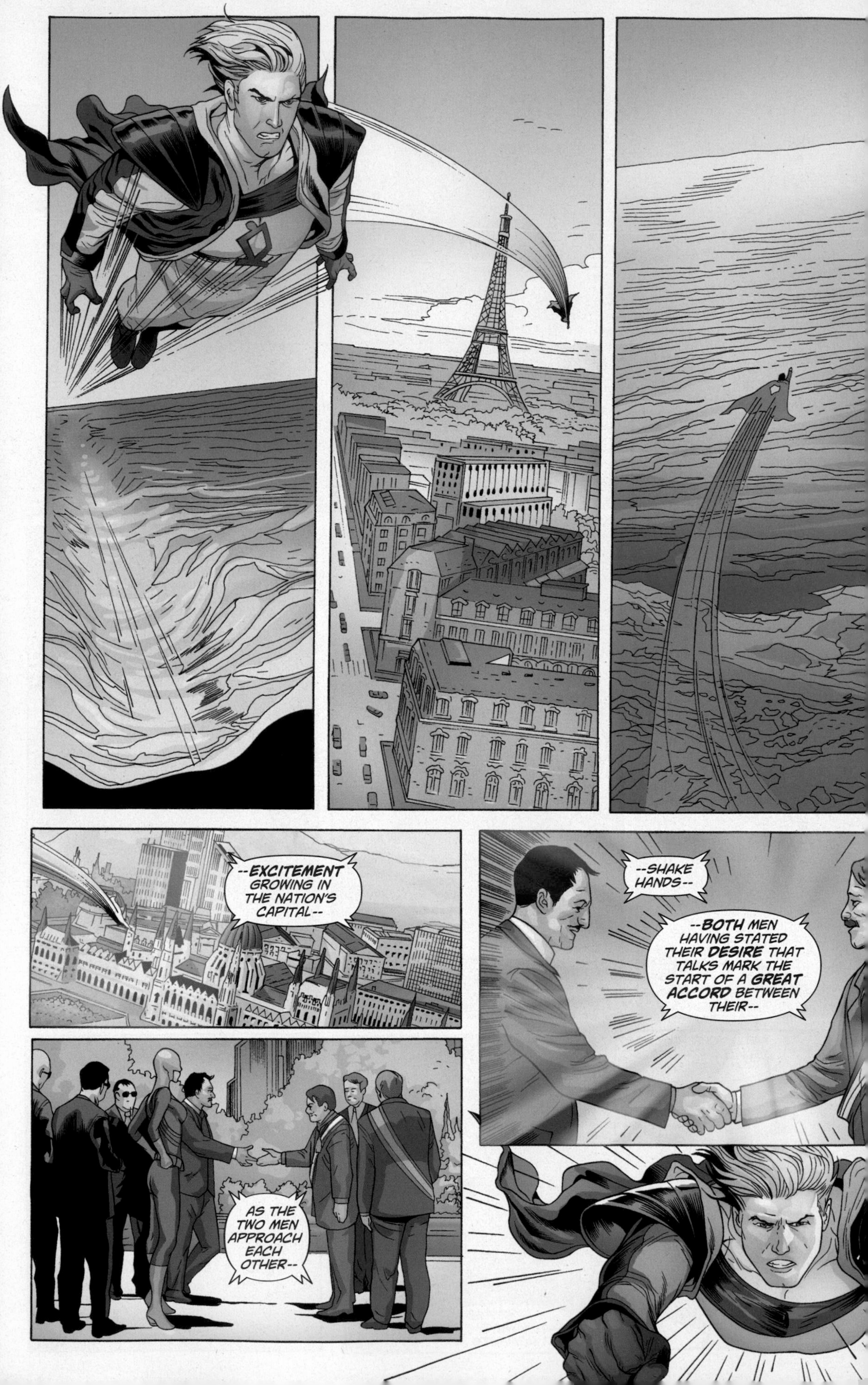
--EXCITEMENT GROWING IN THE NATION'S CAPITAL--
AS THE TWO MEN APPROACH EACH OTHER--
--SHAKE HANDS--
--BOTH MEN HAVING STATED THEIR DESIRE THAT TALKS MARK THE START OF A GREAT ACCORD BETWEEN THEIR--

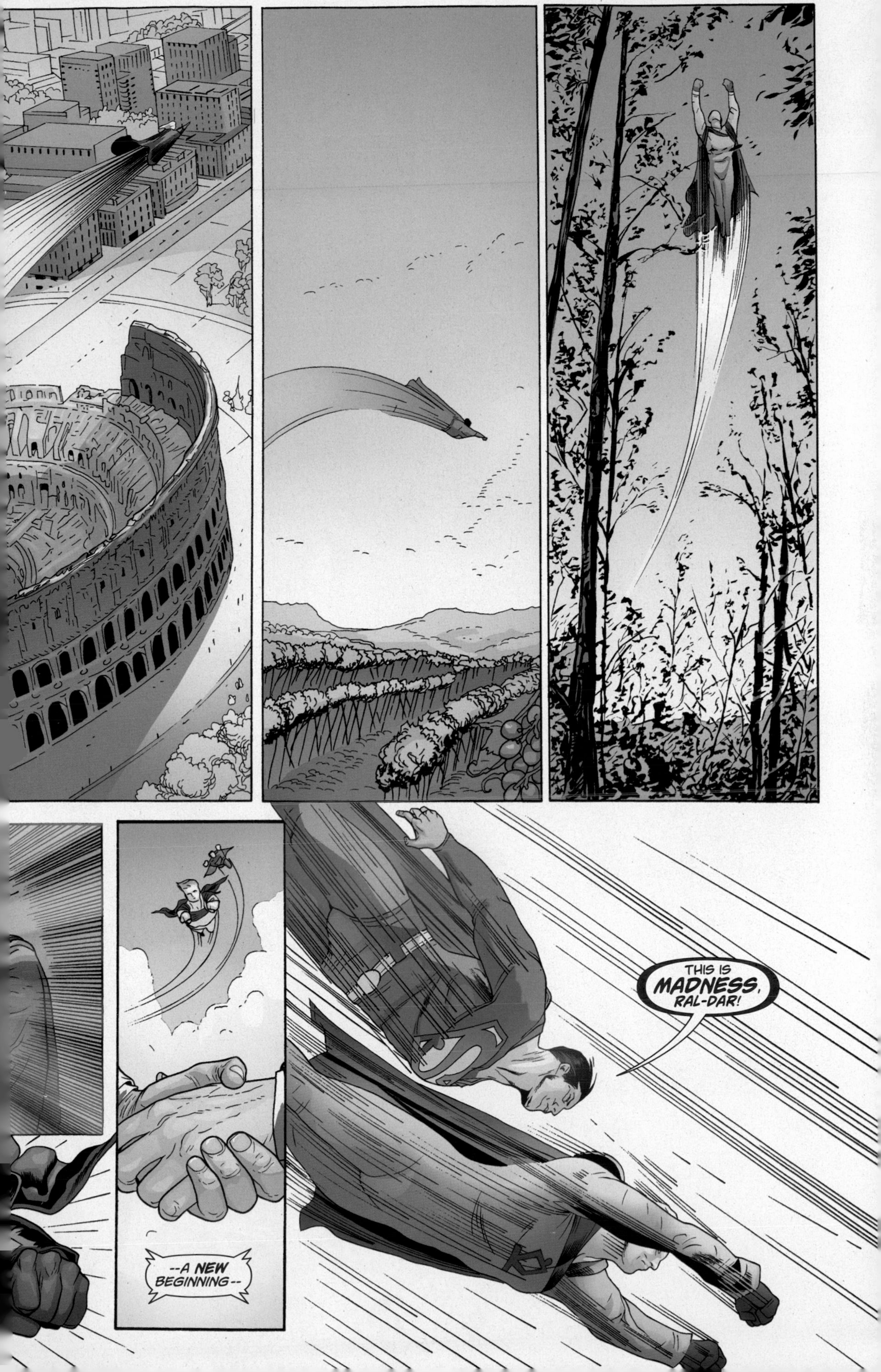
--A NEW BEGINNING--
THIS IS MADNESS, RAL-DAR!

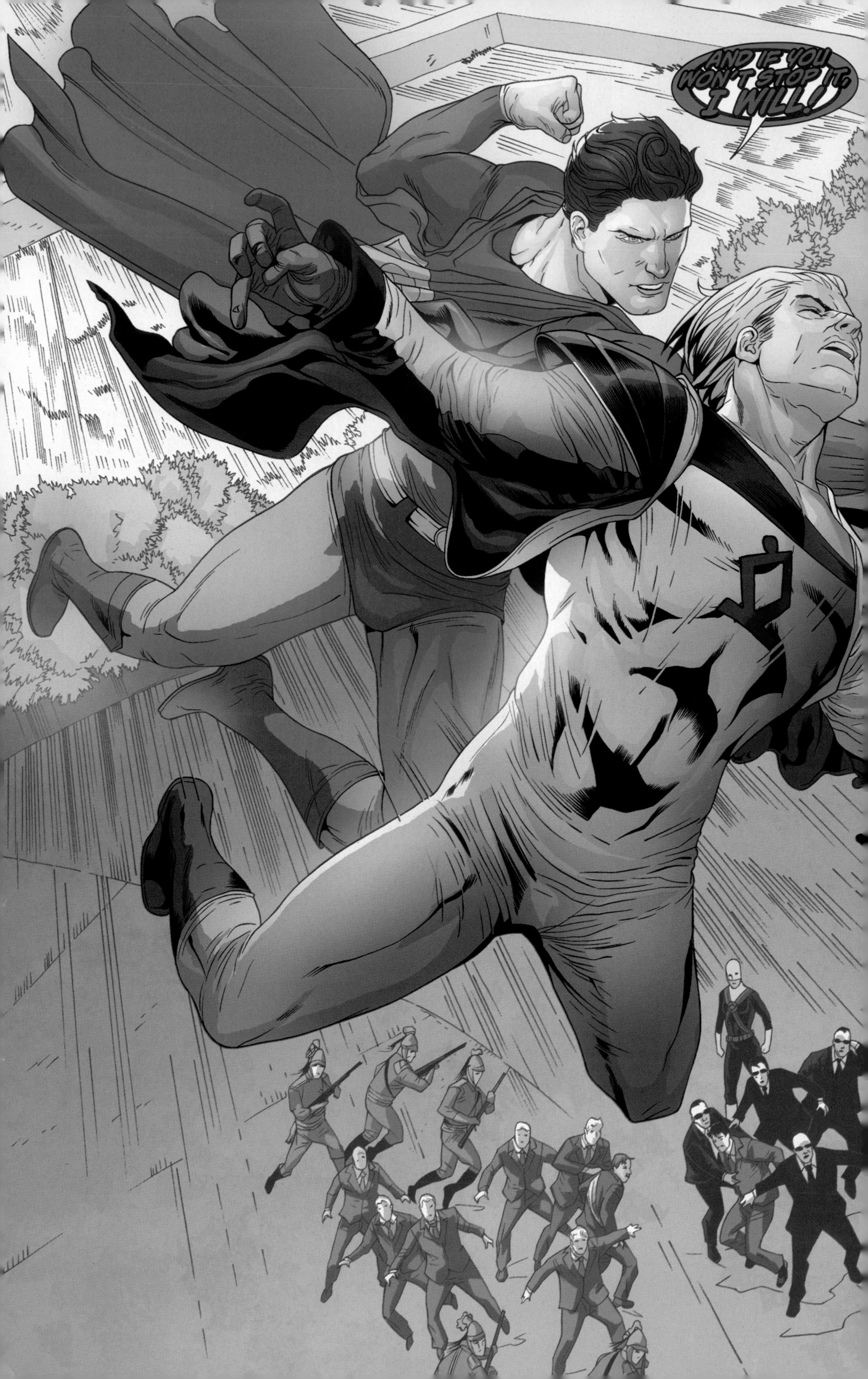
AND IF YOU WON'T STOP IT, I WILL!

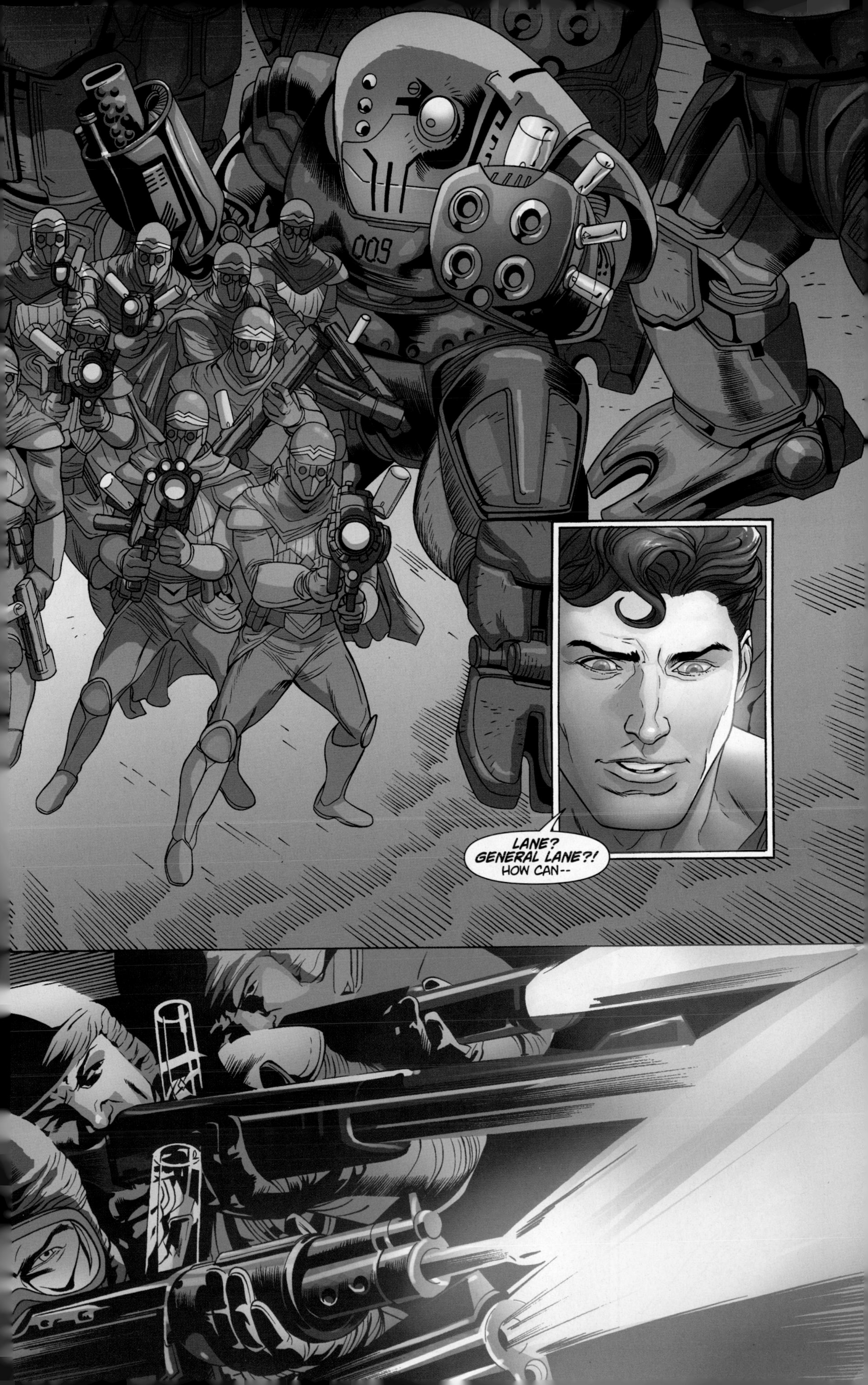
LANE?
GENERAL LANE?!
HOW CAN--

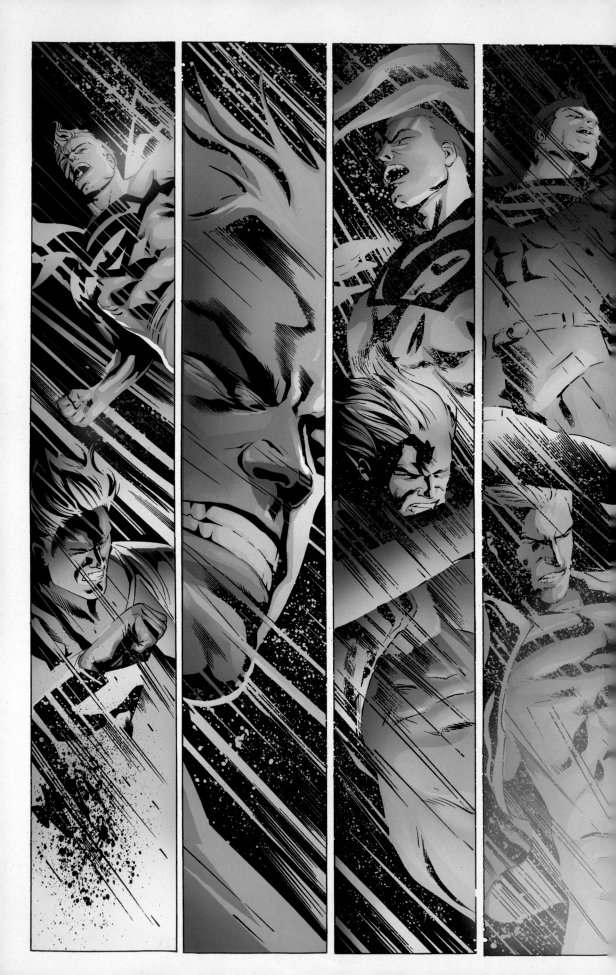

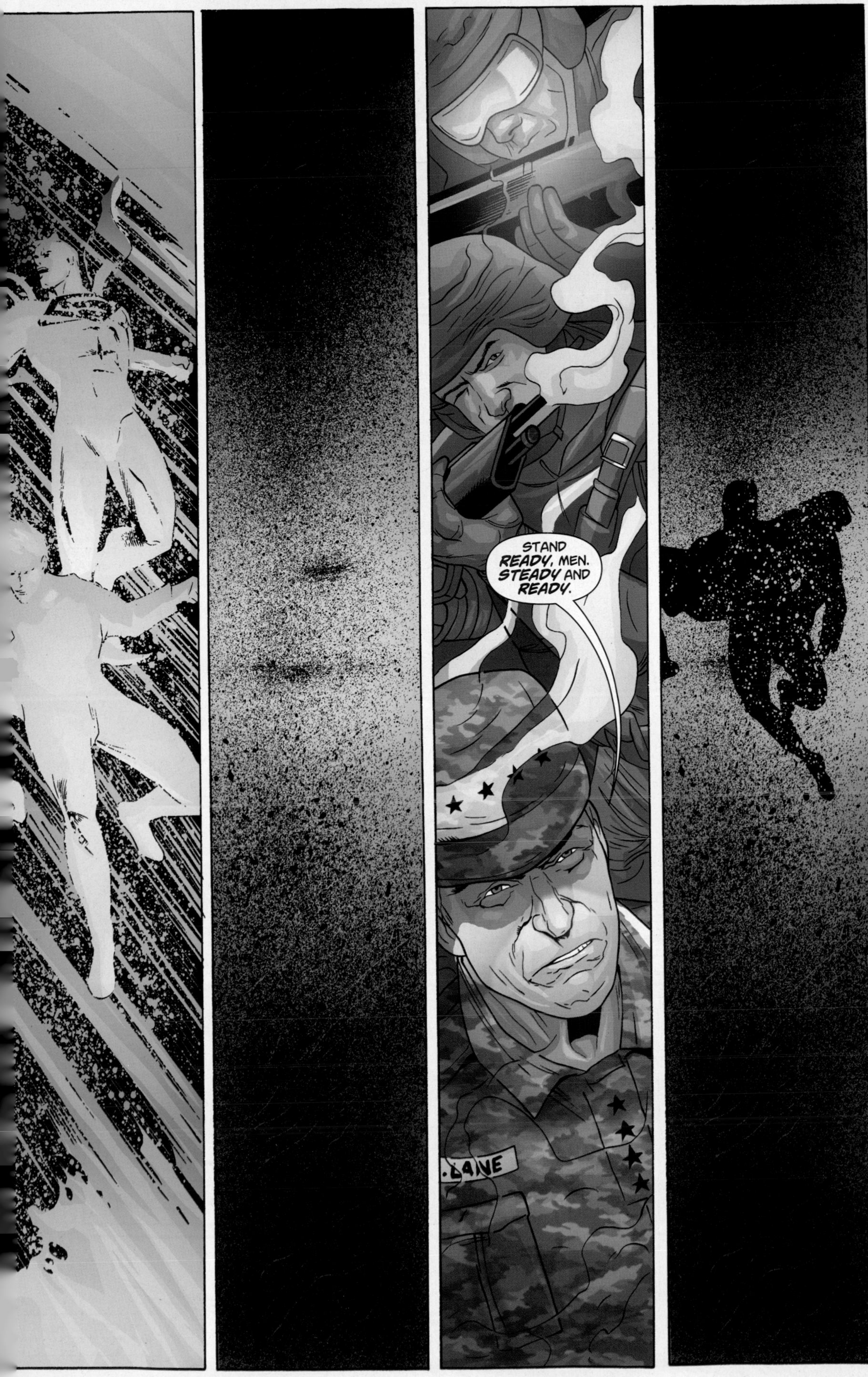
STAND READY, MEN. STEADY AND READY.
.LANE

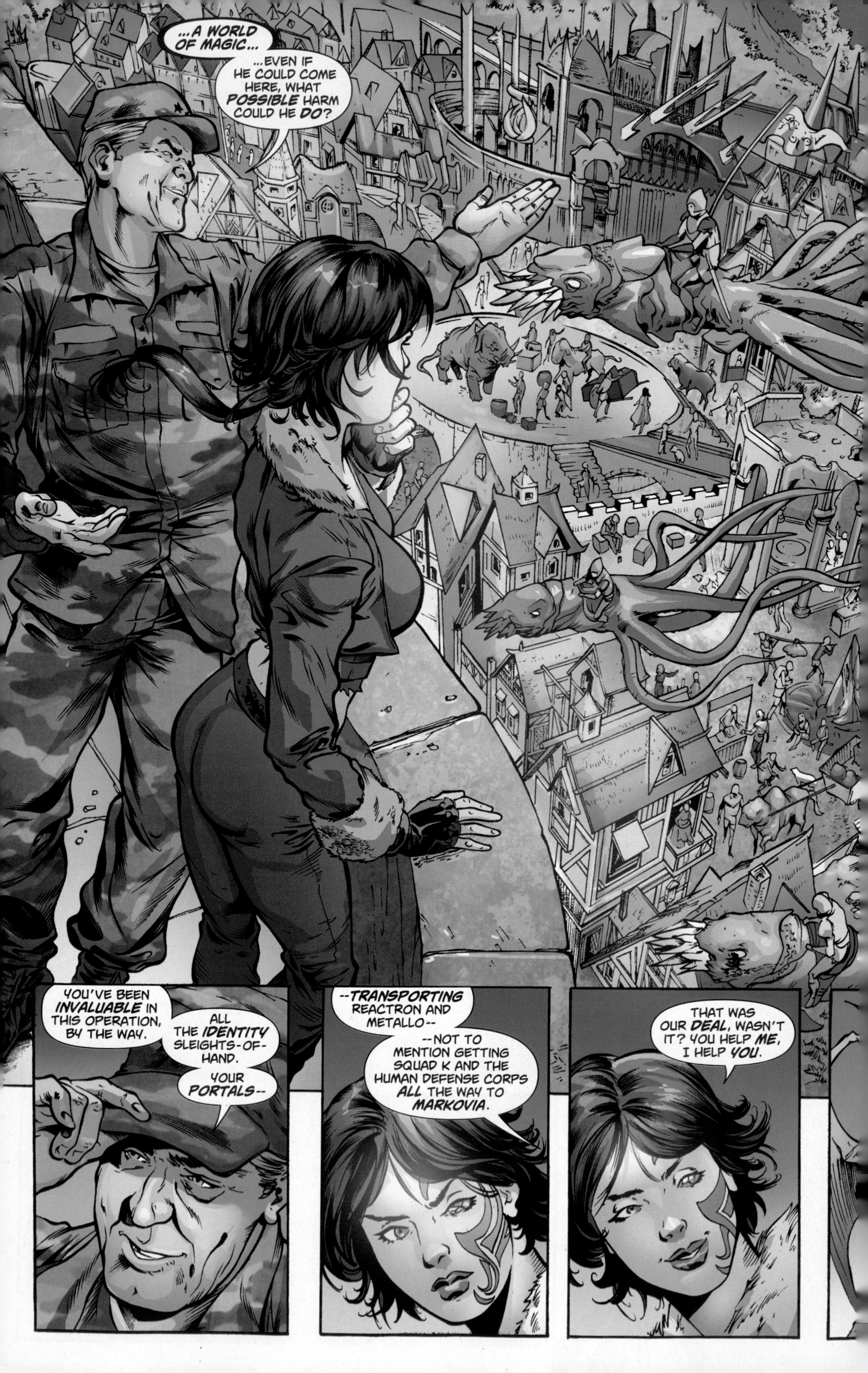
...A WORLD OF MAGIC...
...EVEN IF HE COULD COME HERE, WHAT POSSIBLE HARM COULD HE DO?
YOU'VE BEEN INVALUABLE IN THIS OPERATION, BY THE WAY.
ALL THE IDENTITY SLEIGHTS-OF-HAND.
YOUR PORTALS--
--TRANSPORTING REACTRON AND METALLO--
--NOT TO MENTION GETTING SQUAD K AND THE HUMAN DEFENSE CORPS ALL THE WAY TO MARKOVIA.
THAT WAS OUR DEAL, WASN'T IT? YOU HELP ME, I HELP YOU.

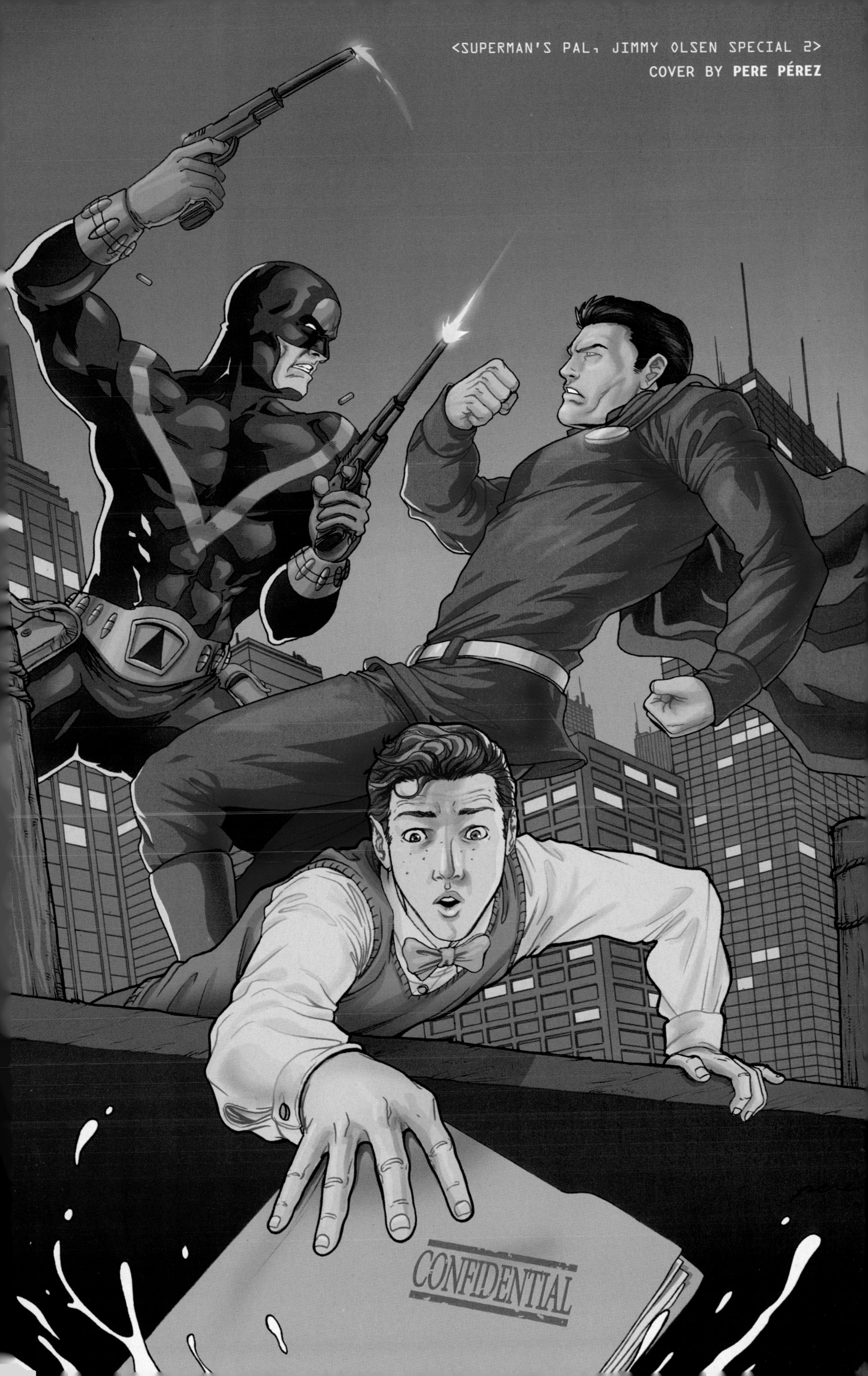
CONFIDENTIAL

<SUPERMAN'S PAL, JIMMY OLSEN SPECIAL 2>
COVER BY **PERE PÉREZ**

CODENAME: PATRIOT <EPILOGUE>

JAMES ROBINSON – WRITER

BERNARD CHANG – ARTIST

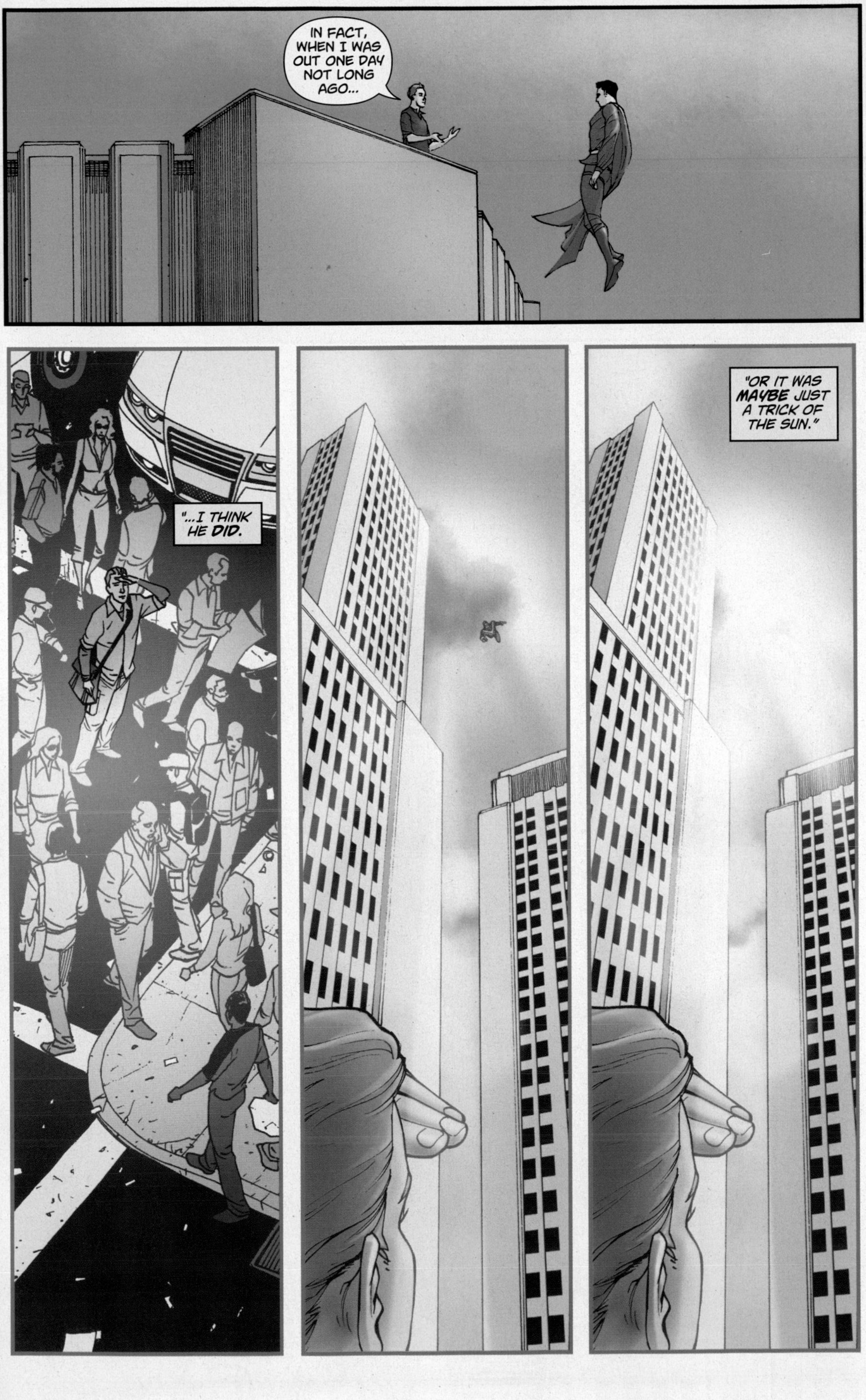
IN FACT, WHEN I WAS OUT ONE DAY NOT LONG AGO...
"...I THINK HE DID.
"OR IT WAS MAYBE JUST A TRICK OF THE SUN."

A WEEK'S GONE BY SINCE MOM AND I HAD OUR CHAT.. THEN SOMETHING-- *SOMEBODY* MAKES THEMSELVES KNOWN.

A GUY ONLINE-- *ETERNITY_7734* HE CALLS HIMSELF. CONSPIRACY *NUTJOB*--SAYS A LOT OF CRAZY STUFF.

RANTS ON ABOUT SOMEONE I'VE NEVER HEARD OF CALLED *KID EMPTY* AND HOW THE GIRL FROM *MARS* SAVED HIM, *WITHOUT* ACTUALLY EXPLAINING WHAT EITHER THING MEANS.

BUT AS HIS NAME INDICATES, HE DOES KNOW ABOUT PROJECT 7734. ALSO SOMETHING CALLED *PROJECT BREACH,* RANTS ABOUT HOW 7734 HAS CONTROL OF THIS "PLANET KILLER" BUT AGAIN *WON'T* GO INTO THE HOW OR WHY.

IT TAKES A *DAY* OF BACK-AND-FORTH I.M.-ING TO WIN HIS TRUST.

HE TELLS ME *WHERE* HE LIVES.

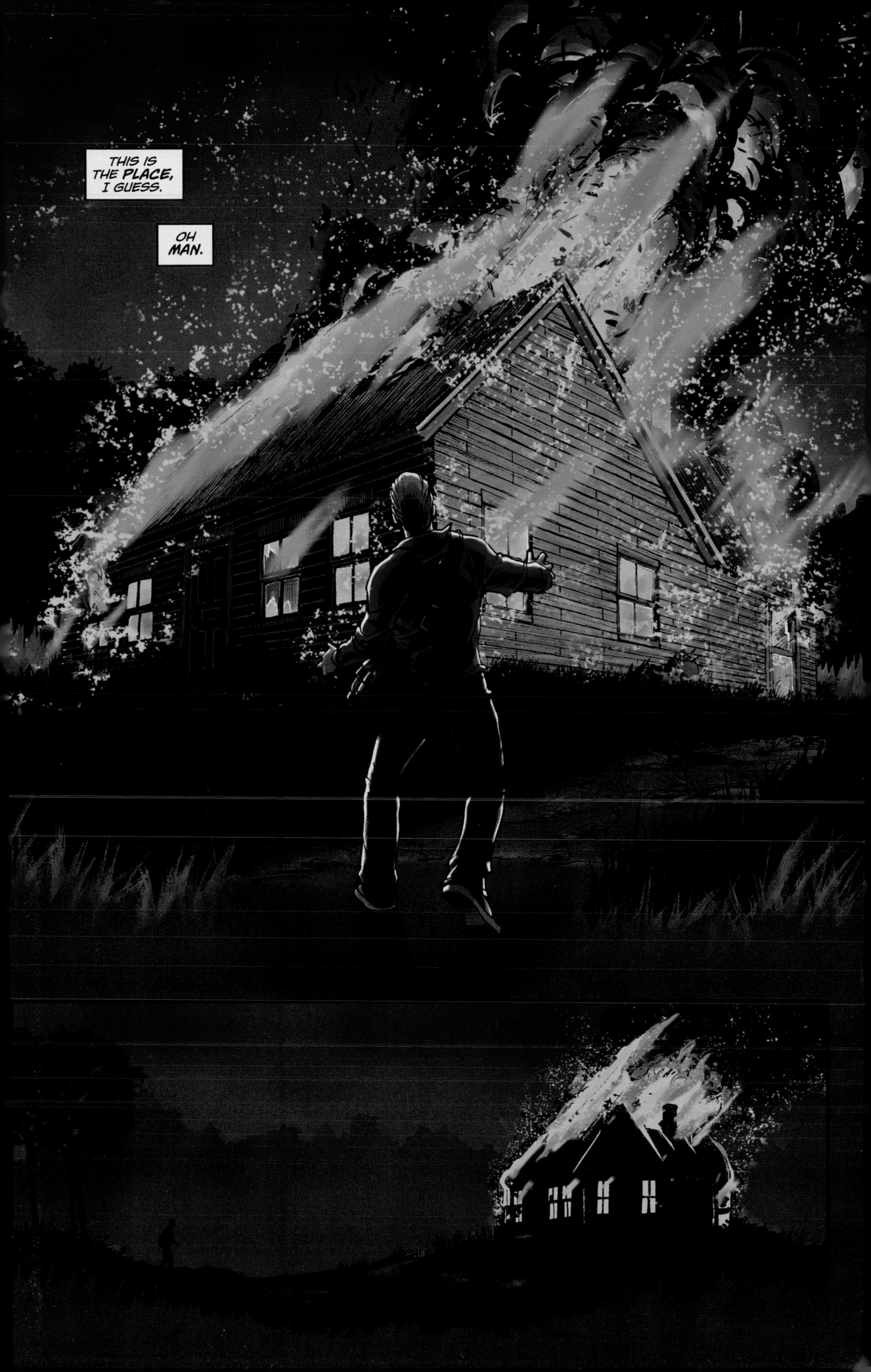
THIS IS THE PLACE, I GUESS.
OH MAN.

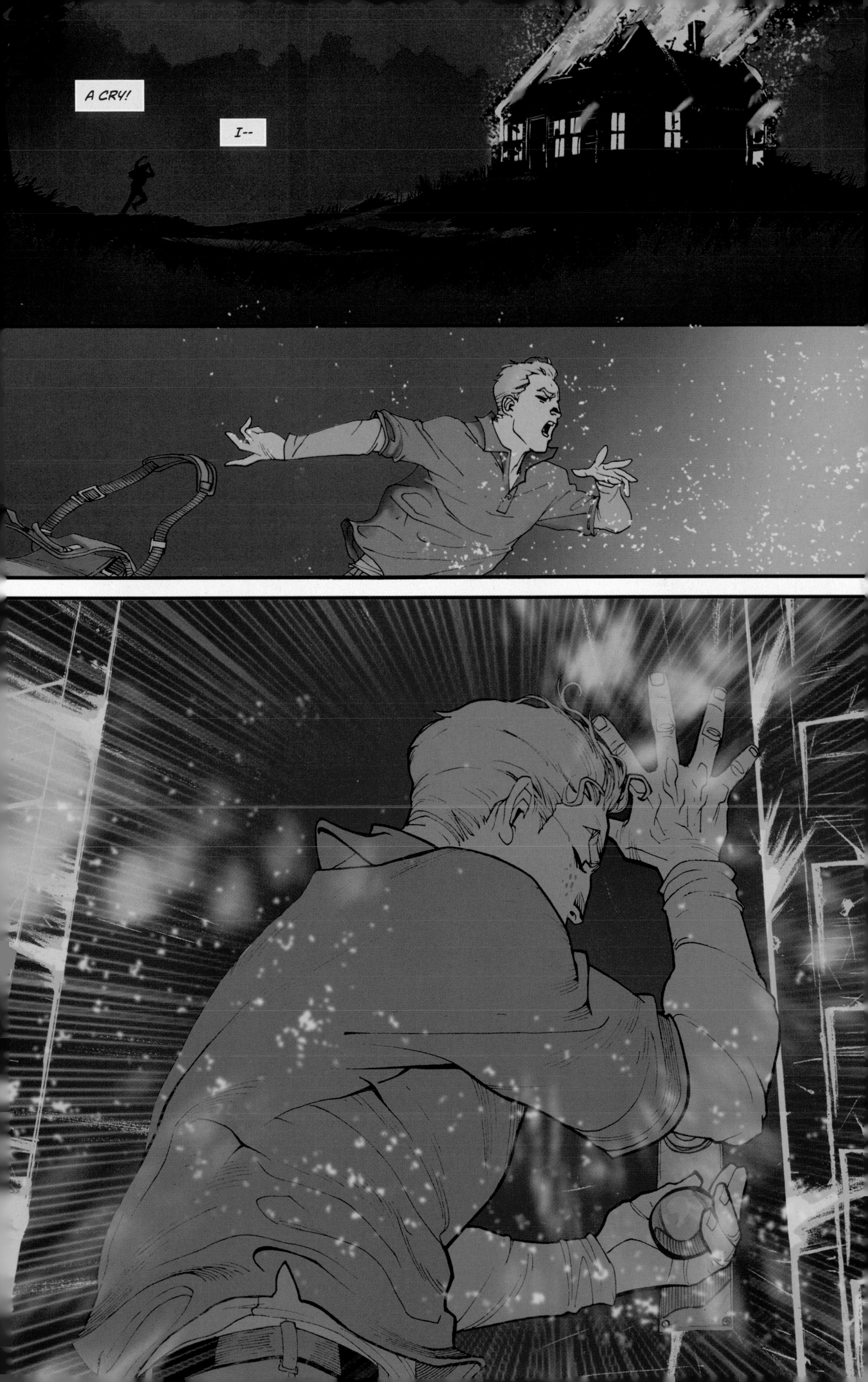
A CRY!
I--

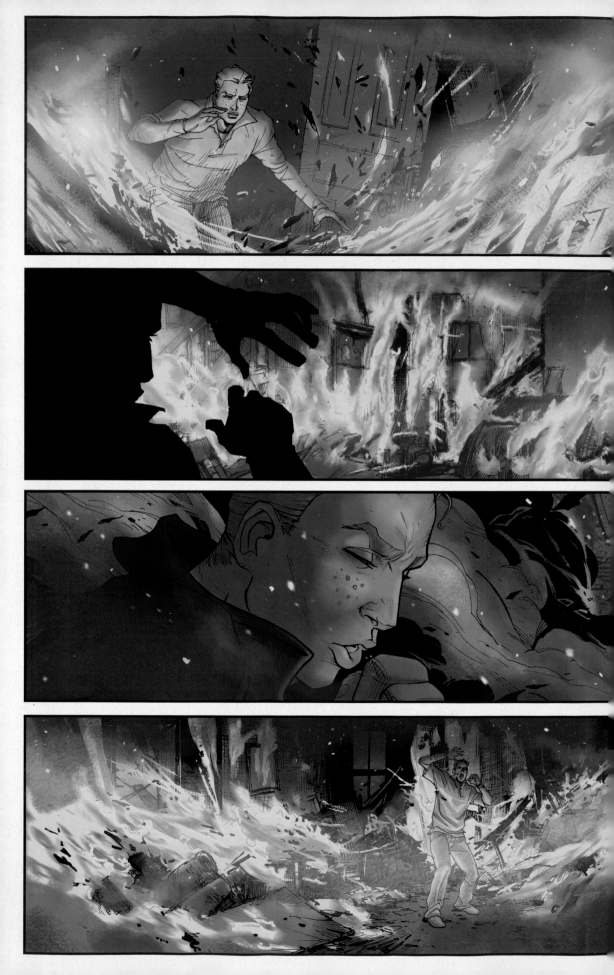

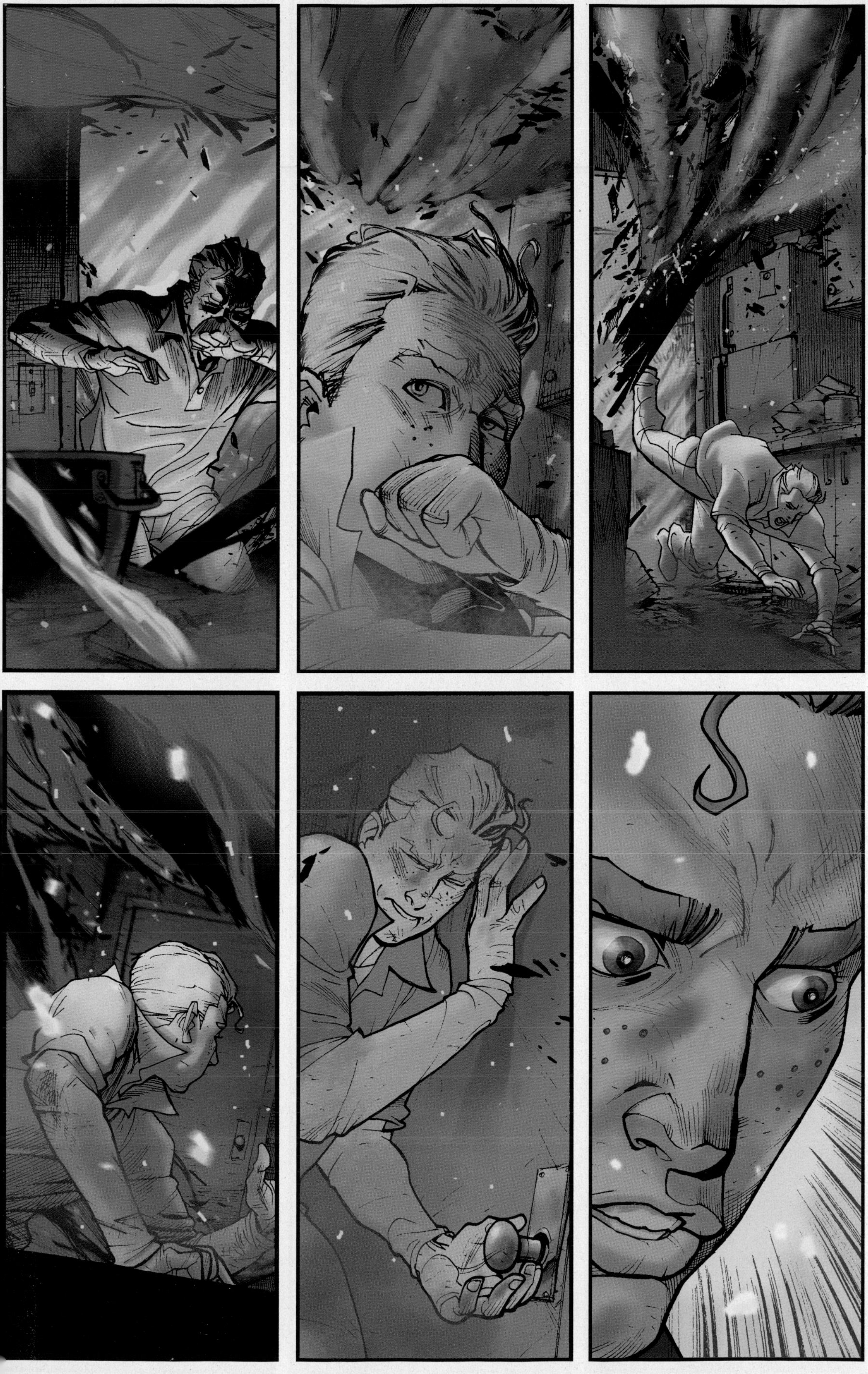

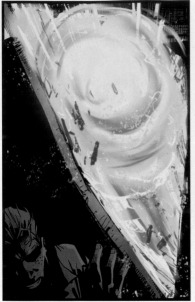

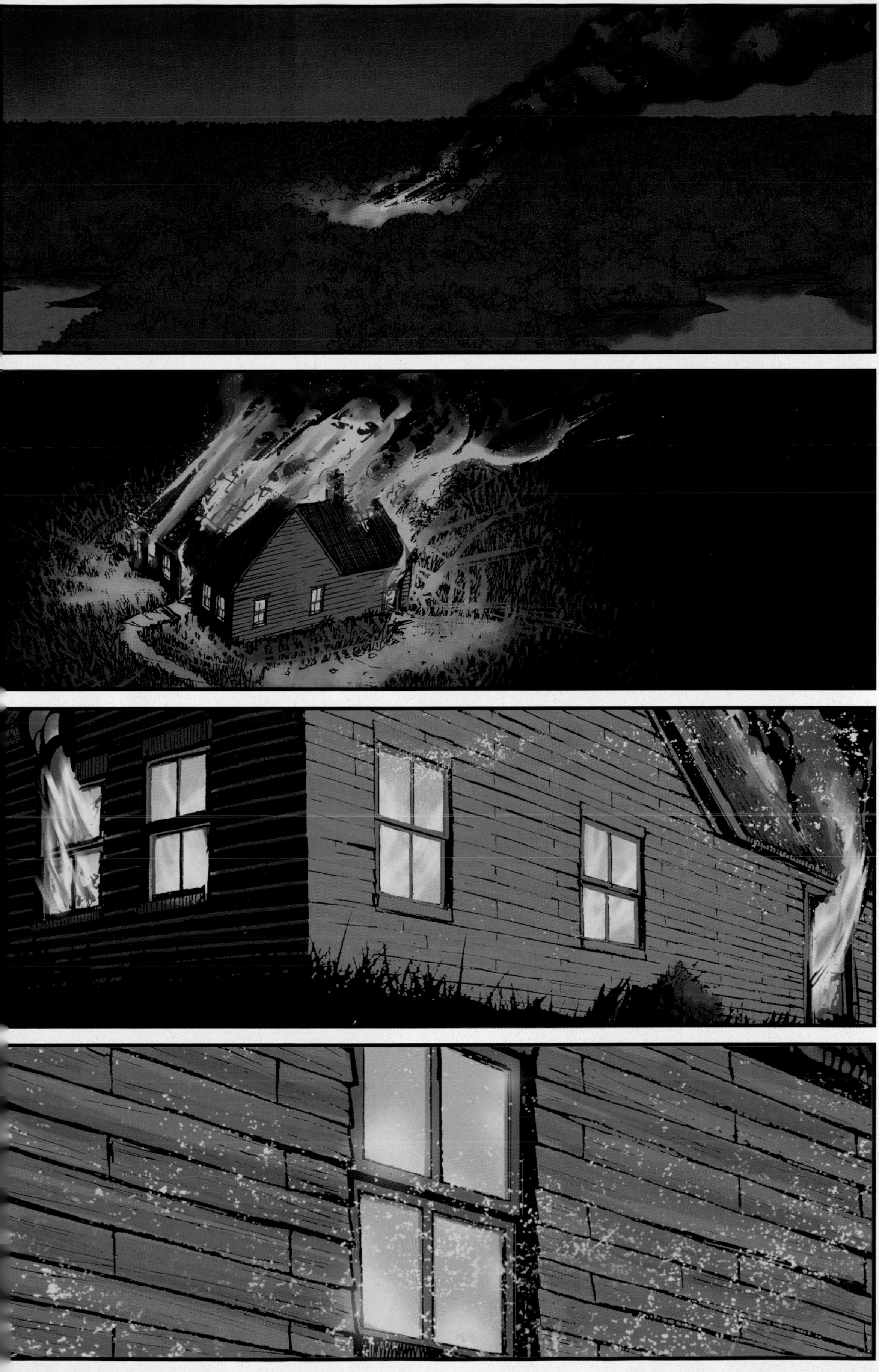

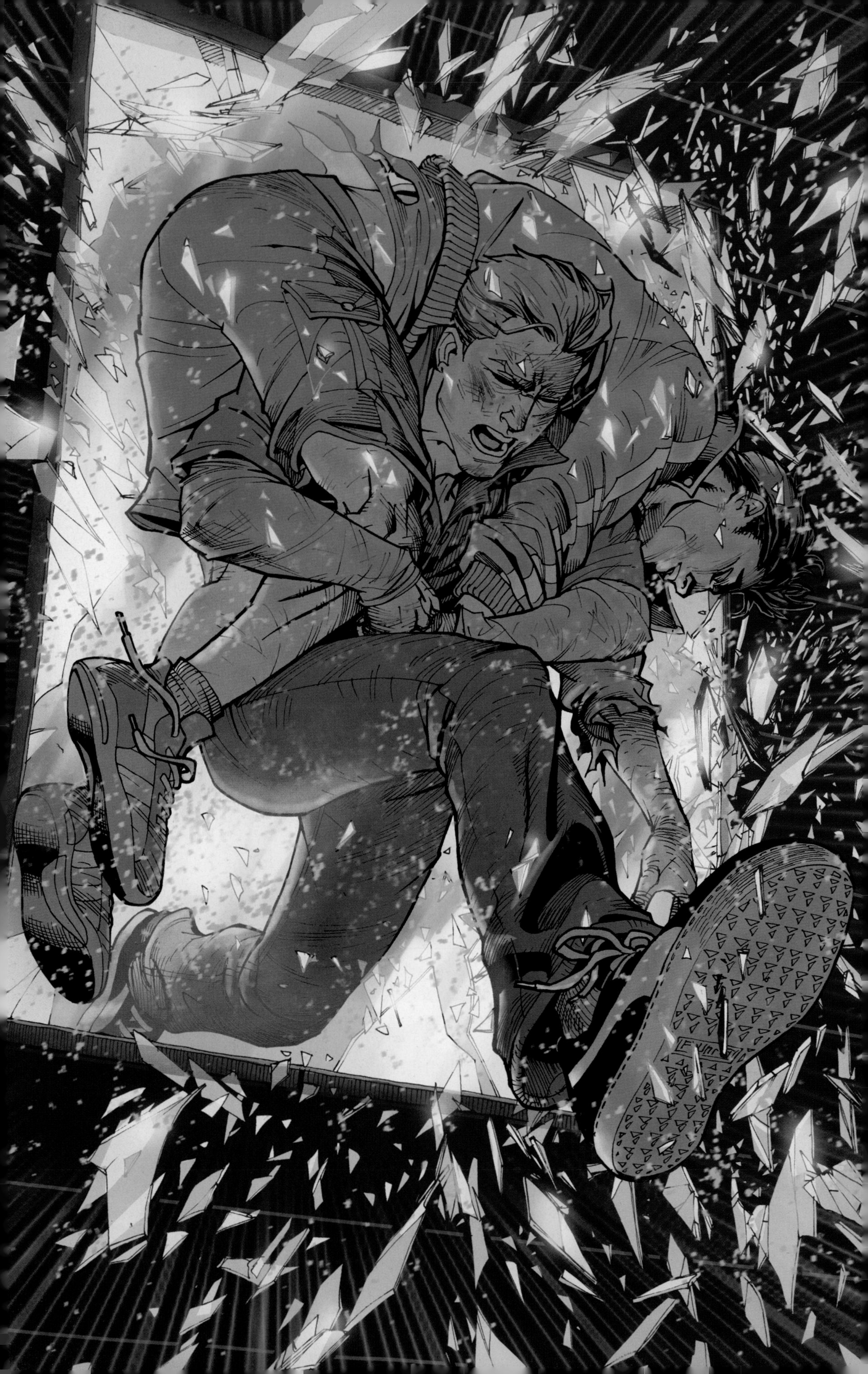

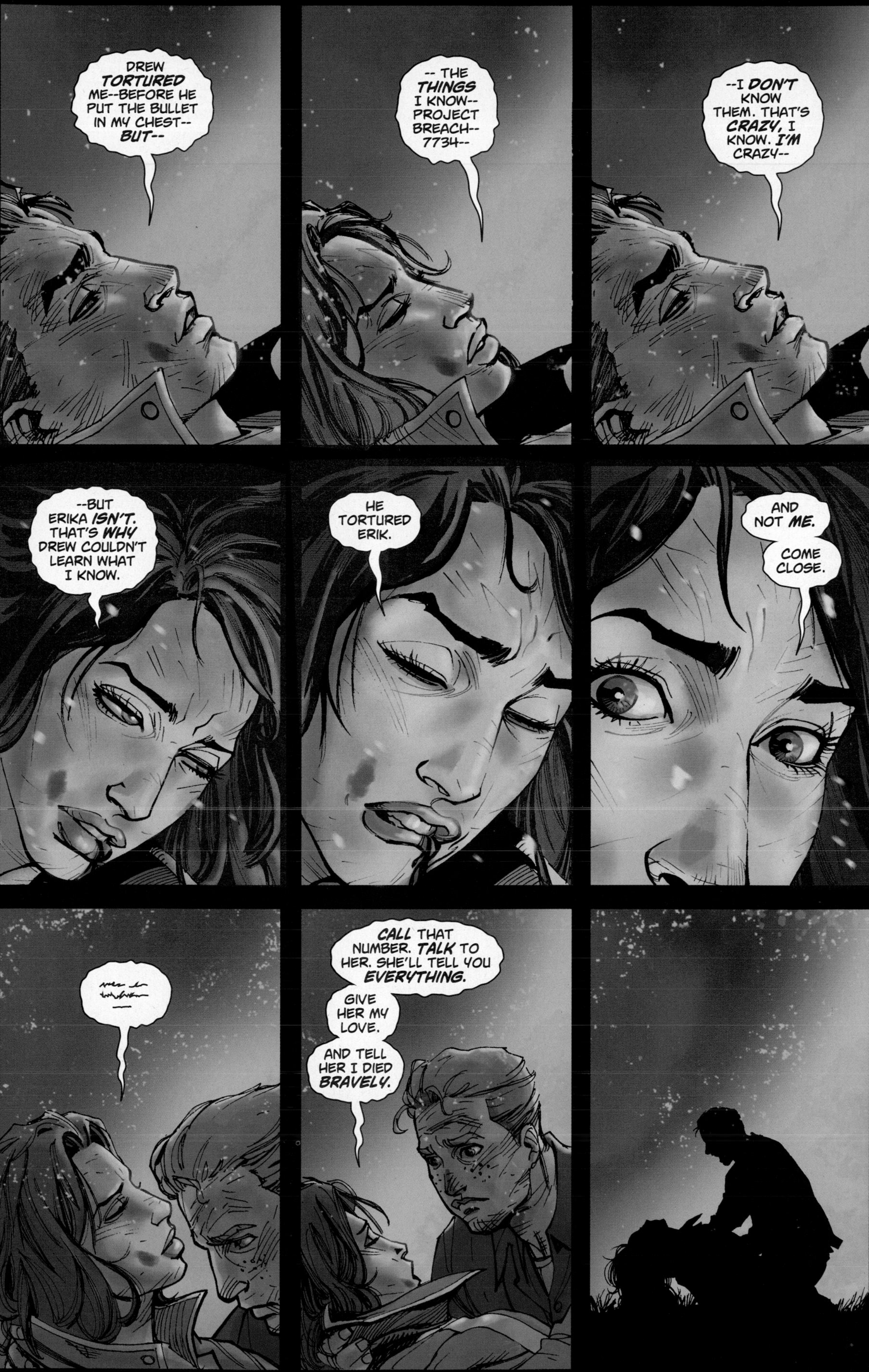
DREW TORTURED ME--BEFORE HE PUT THE BULLET IN MY CHEST-- BUT--
-- THE THINGS I KNOW-- PROJECT BREACH-- 7734--
--I DON'T KNOW THEM. THAT'S CRAZY, I KNOW. I'M CRAZY--
--BUT ERIKA ISN'T. THAT'S WHY DREW COULDN'T LEARN WHAT I KNOW.
HE TORTURED ERIK.
AND NOT ME.
COME CLOSE.
CALL THAT NUMBER. TALK TO HER. SHE'LL TELL YOU EVERYTHING.
GIVE HER MY LOVE.
AND TELL HER I DIED BRAVELY.

'COURSE GOD FORBID SHE PICKS A PLACE IN METROPOLIS.

I SUGGEST THAT, IN FACT, AND SHE REPLIES, "ANYWHERE BUT."

SO A LONG DAY'S PLANE RIDE AND I'M IN RIVER CITY. NO HEROES TO SPEAK OF. THE ODD MAN. THAT'S IT.

THEN AGAIN, THERE'S NOT MUCH CRIME HERE TO SPEAK OF, EITHER.

BUT IT IS NIGHT, SO BASED ON THE "CREEPY QUOTIENT," IT MIGHT AS WELL BE A GRAVEYARD.

I CAN HEAR THE HARBOR WATERS NOT TOO FAR OFF, WHICH ISN'T HELPING, EITHER--

HELLO, JIMMY...

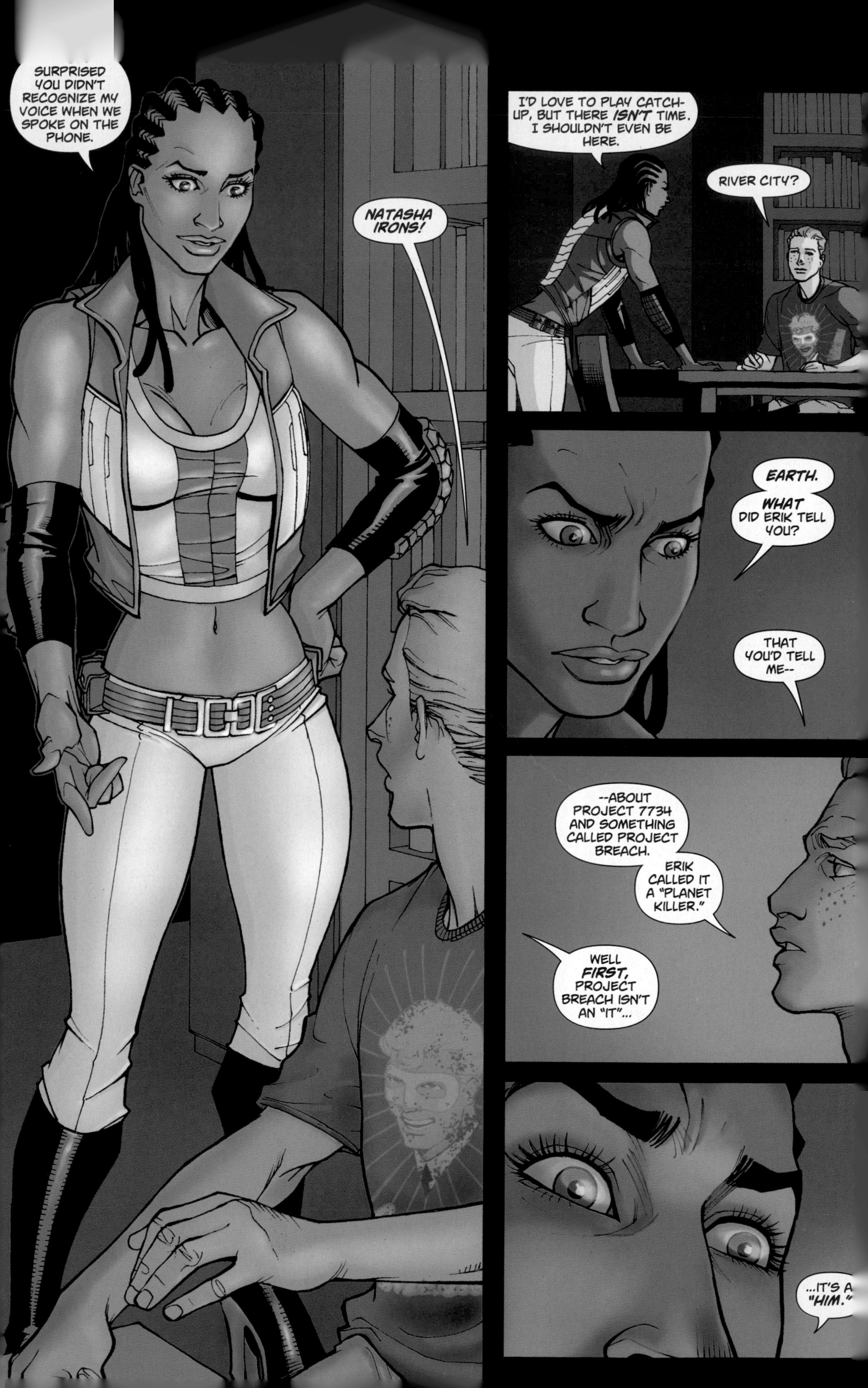

SURPRISED YOU DIDN'T RECOGNIZE MY VOICE WHEN WE SPOKE ON THE PHONE.
NATASHA IRONS!
I'D LOVE TO PLAY CATCH-UP, BUT THERE ISN'T TIME. I SHOULDN'T EVEN BE HERE.
RIVER CITY?
EARTH.
WHAT DID ERIK TELL YOU?
THAT YOU'D TELL ME--
--ABOUT PROJECT 7734 AND SOMETHING CALLED PROJECT BREACH.
ERIK CALLED IT A "PLANET KILLER."
WELL FIRST, PROJECT BREACH ISN'T AN "IT"...
...IT'S A "HIM."

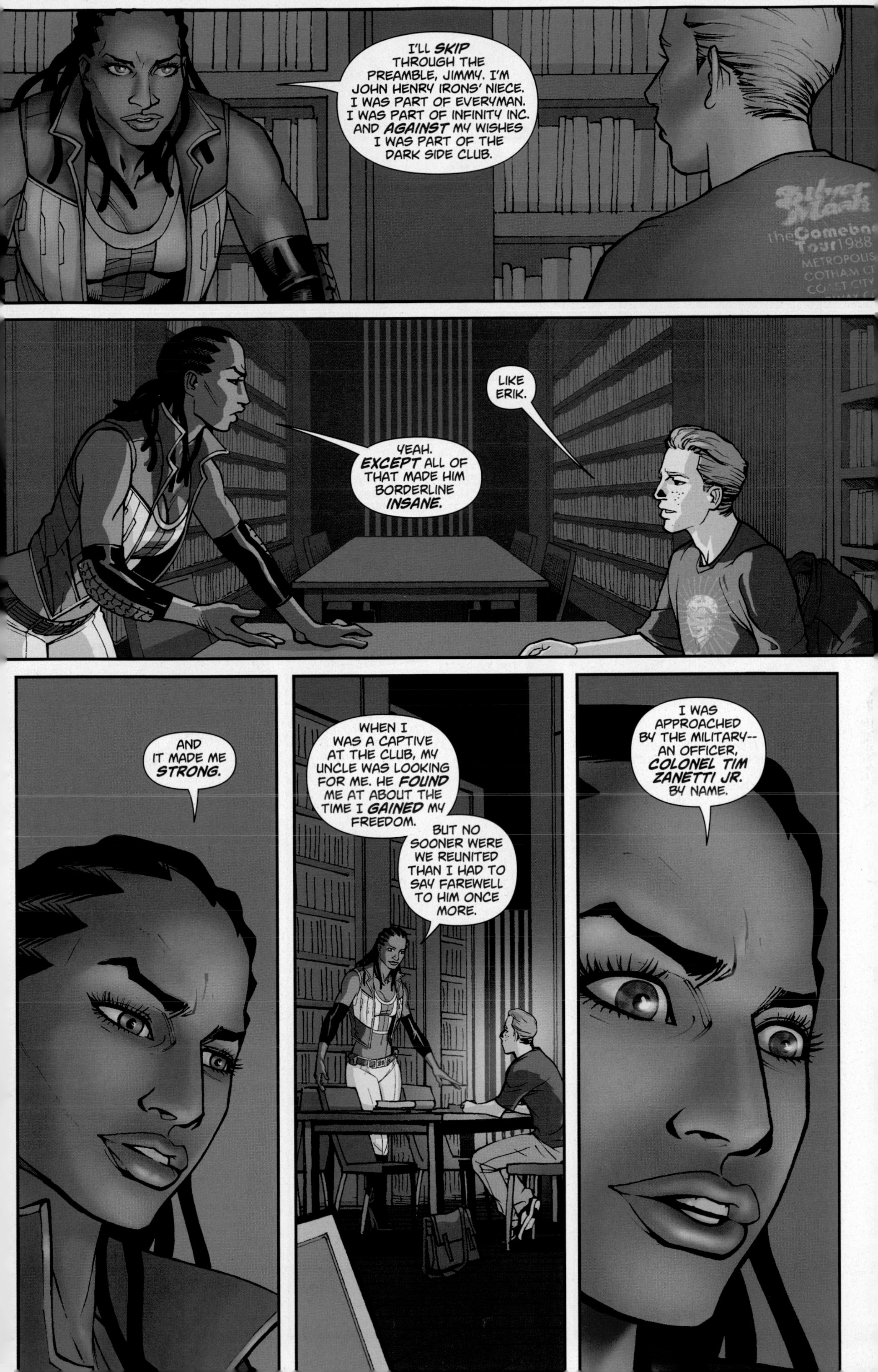
I'LL **SKIP** THROUGH THE PREAMBLE, JIMMY. I'M JOHN HENRY IRONS' NIECE. I WAS PART OF EVERYMAN. I WAS PART OF INFINITY INC. AND **AGAINST** MY WISHES I WAS PART OF THE DARK SIDE CLUB.
METROPOLIS
COAST CITY
LIKE ERIK.
YEAH. **EXCEPT** ALL OF THAT MADE HIM BORDERLINE **INSANE.**
AND IT MADE ME **STRONG.**
WHEN I WAS A CAPTIVE AT THE CLUB, MY UNCLE WAS LOOKING FOR ME. HE **FOUND** ME AT ABOUT THE TIME I **GAINED** MY FREEDOM.
BUT NO SOONER WERE WE REUNITED THAN I HAD TO SAY FAREWELL TO HIM ONCE MORE.
I WAS APPROACHED BY THE MILITARY-- AN OFFICER, **COLONEL TIM ZANETTI JR.** BY NAME.

"HIS FATHER, TIM SR., HAD BEEN A PART OF AN EXPERIMENT TWENTY YEARS AGO--

"--THAT ENDED WITH HIM BECOMING THE ATOMIC CREATURE KNOWN AS BREACH."

THAT'S WHAT TIM RECRUITED ME TO FIND OUT. THE **OFFICIAL** STORY IS THAT BREACH BLEW UP DURING ONE OF THE "CRISISES". TIM JR. WANTED TO KNOW IF HIS FATHER STILL BREATHED.

AND **THAT'S** WHAT 7734 HAS?

AND **DOES** HE?

NO. BREACH IS **DEFINITELY** DEAD.

7734-- OR RATHER ITS **LEADER**--HAS A THING FOR WORD PUZZLES AND PUNS AND SUCH. HE THOUGHT IT WAS **FUNNY** THAT BREACH'S ORIGIN SO CLOSELY PARALLELED HIS **ACTUAL** TEST SUBJECT.

SO **NOT** TIM ZANETTI SR.?

NO. **CAPTAIN NATHANIEL ADAM**. BETTER KNOWN TO YOU AND EVERYONE AS...

...CAPTAIN ATOM.

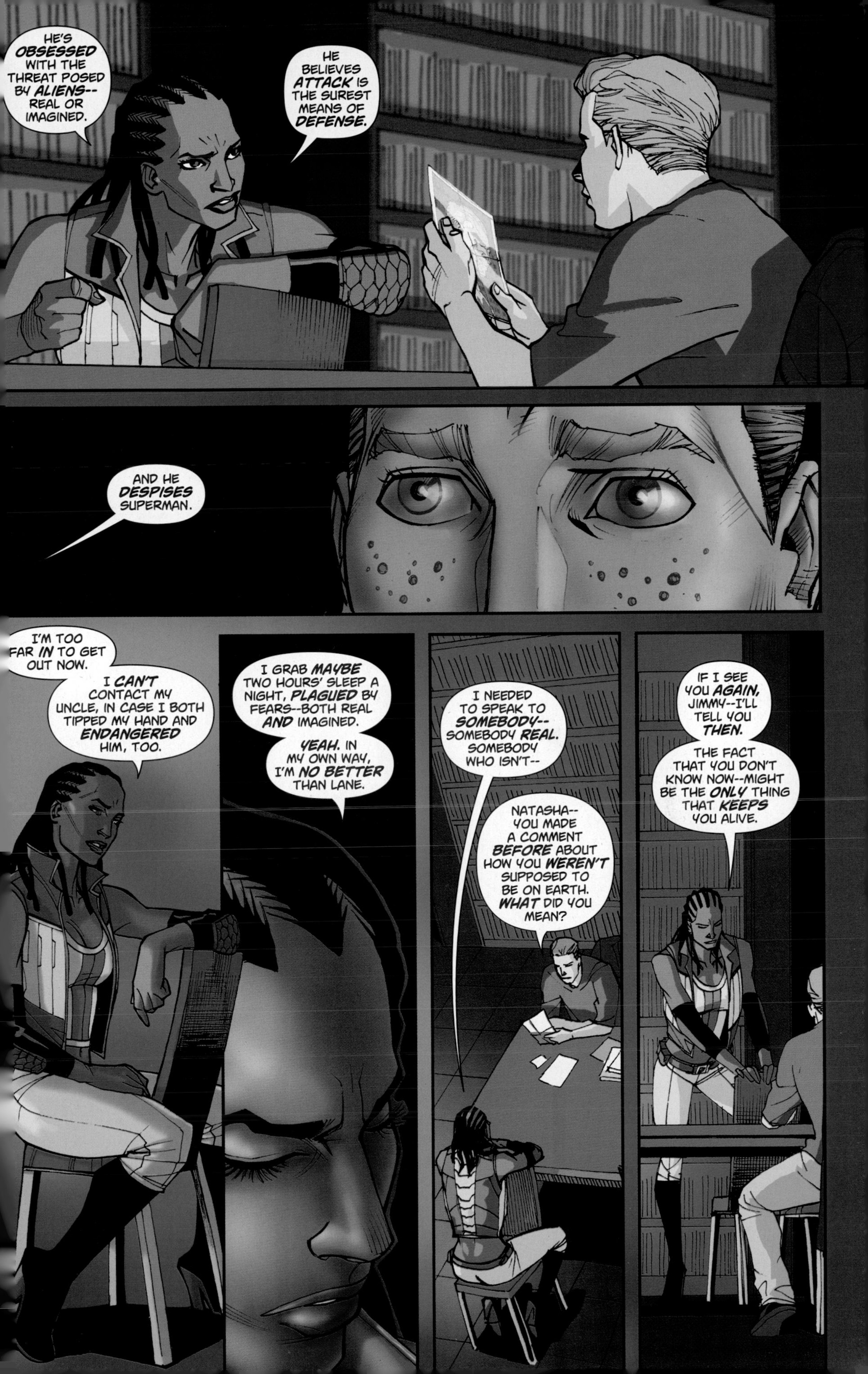
HE'S OBSESSED WITH THE THREAT POSED BY ALIENS-- REAL OR IMAGINED.
HE BELIEVES ATTACK IS THE SUREST MEANS OF DEFENSE.
AND HE DESPISES SUPERMAN.
I'M TOO FAR IN TO GET OUT NOW.
I CAN'T CONTACT MY UNCLE, IN CASE I BOTH TIPPED MY HAND AND ENDANGERED HIM, TOO.
I GRAB MAYBE TWO HOURS' SLEEP A NIGHT, PLAGUED BY FEARS--BOTH REAL AND IMAGINED.
YEAH. IN MY OWN WAY, I'M NO BETTER THAN LANE.
I NEEDED TO SPEAK TO SOMEBODY-- SOMEBODY REAL. SOMEBODY WHO ISN'T--
NATASHA-- YOU MADE A COMMENT BEFORE ABOUT HOW YOU WEREN'T SUPPOSED TO BE ON EARTH. WHAT DID YOU MEAN?
IF I SEE YOU AGAIN, JIMMY--I'LL TELL YOU THEN.
THE FACT THAT YOU DON'T KNOW NOW--MIGHT BE THE ONLY THING THAT KEEPS YOU ALIVE.

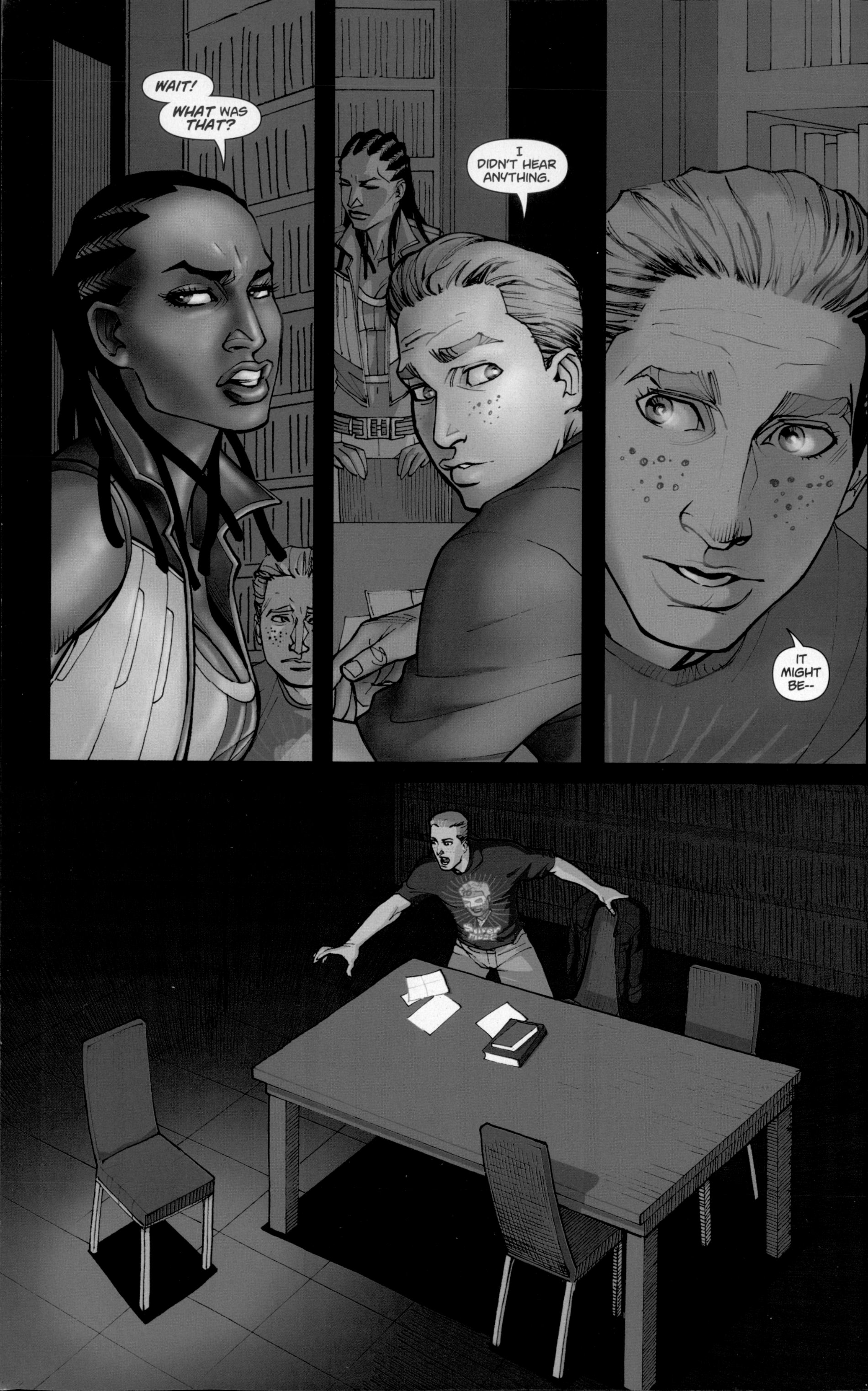
WAIT! WHAT WAS THAT?
I DIDN'T HEAR ANYTHING.
IT MIGHT BE--

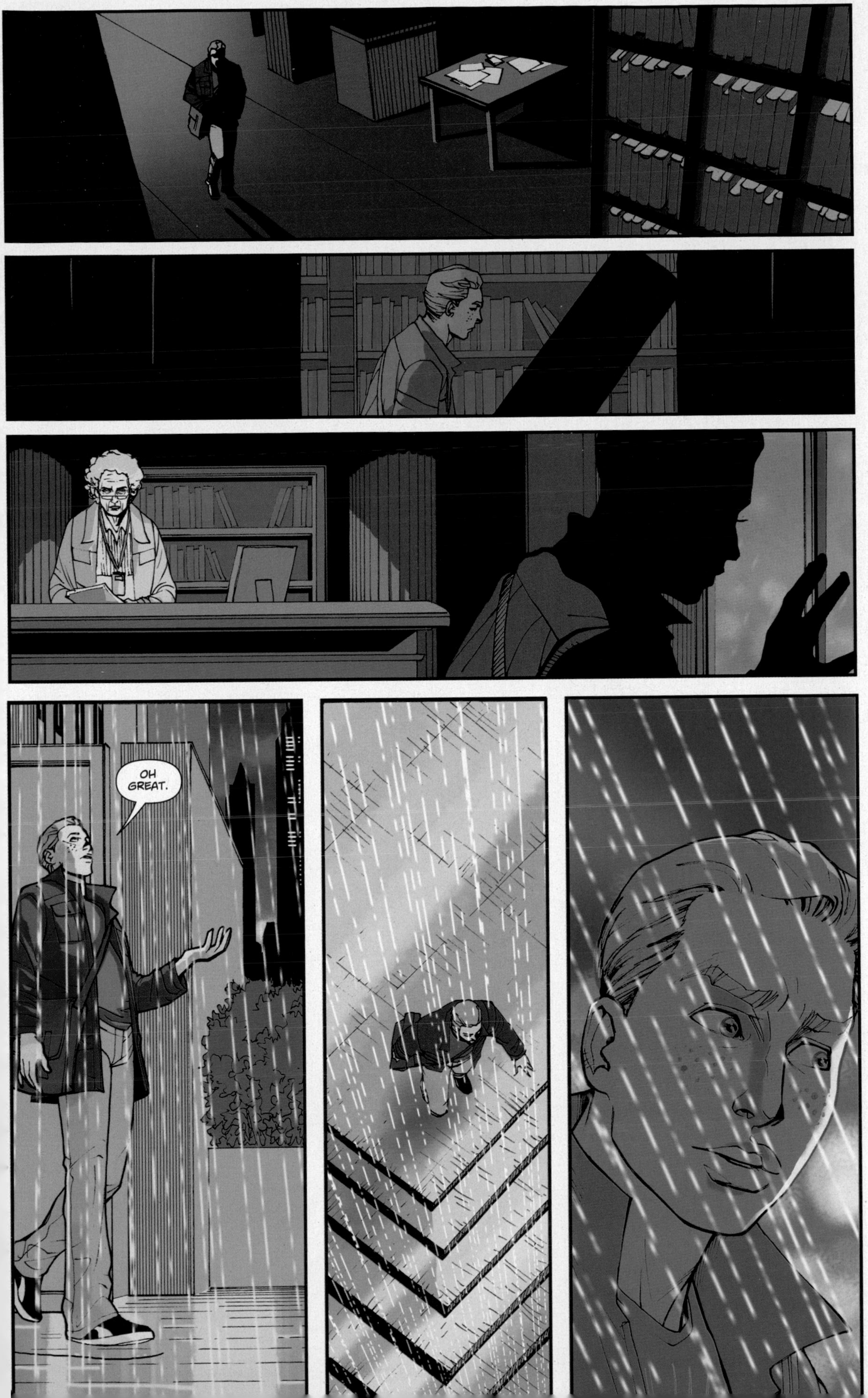
OH GREAT.

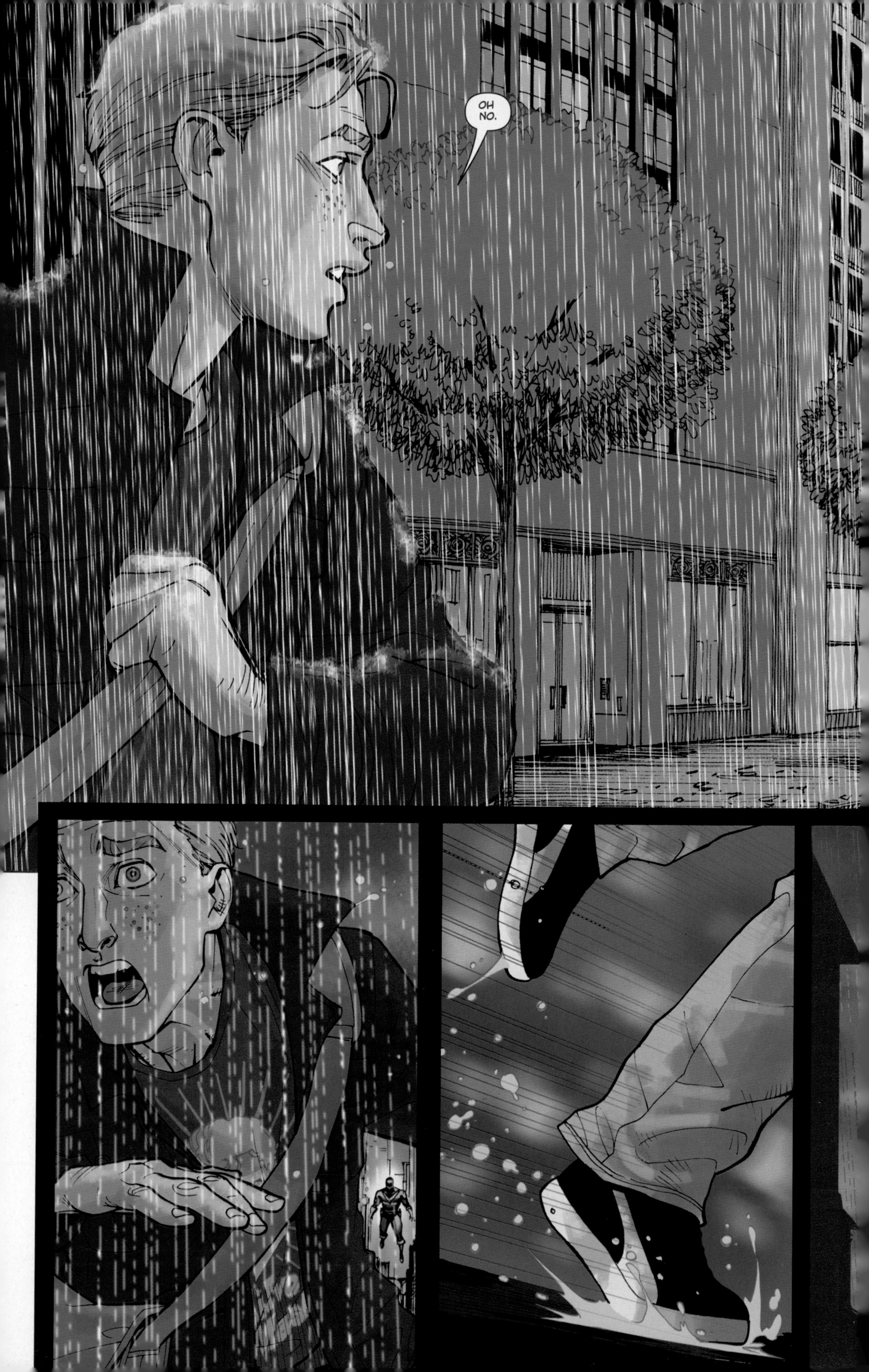
OH NO.

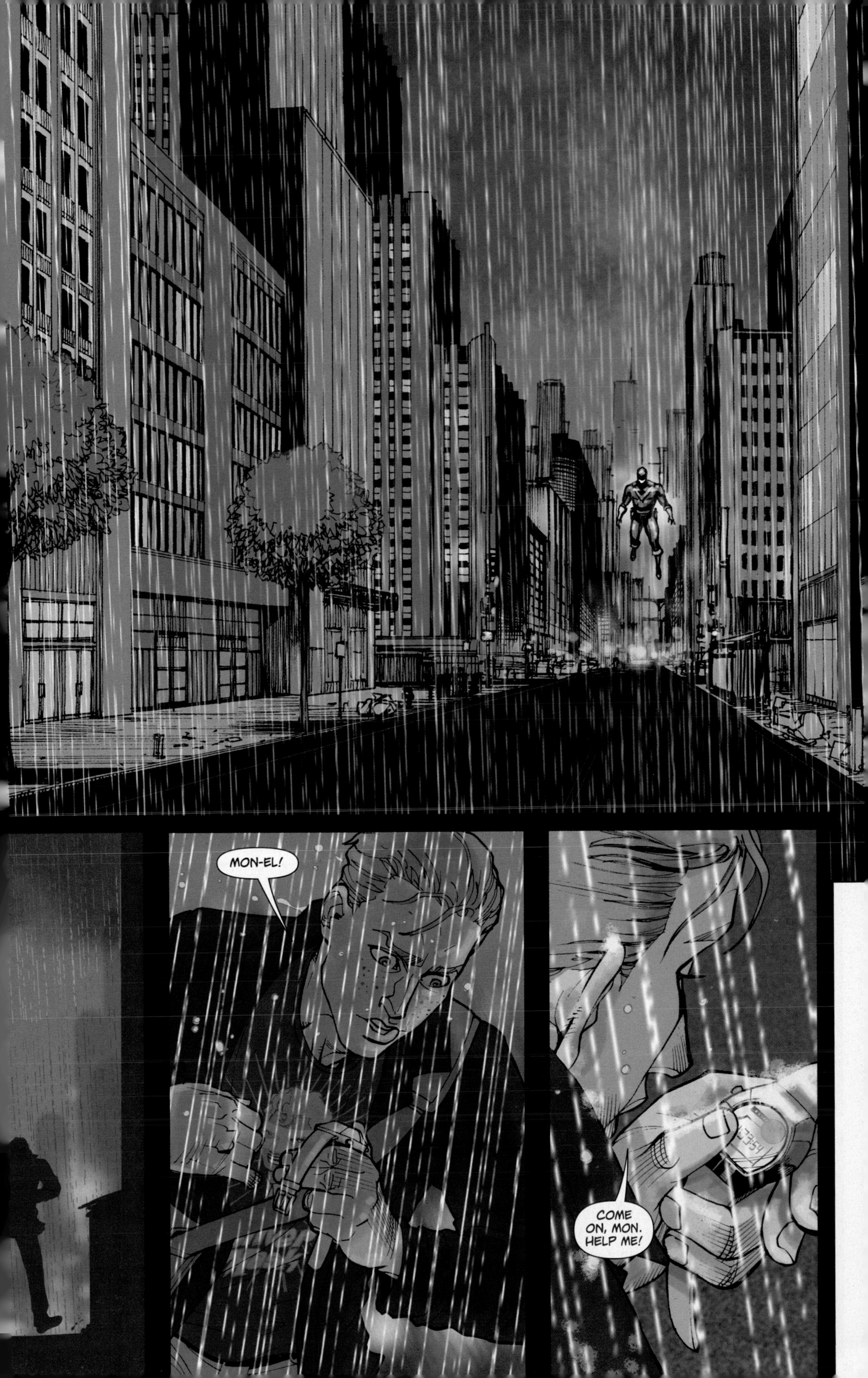
MON-EL!
COME ON, MON. HELP ME!

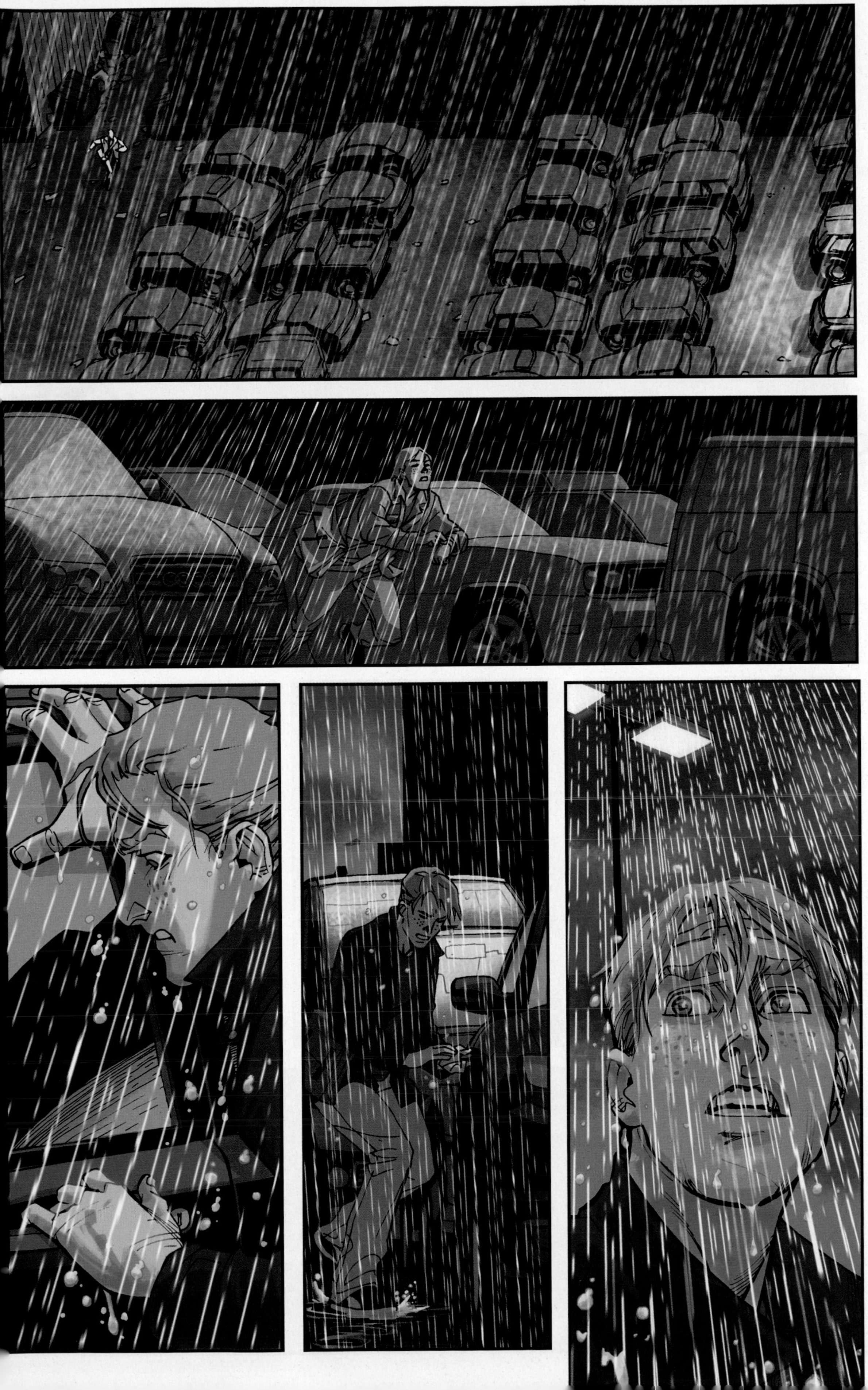

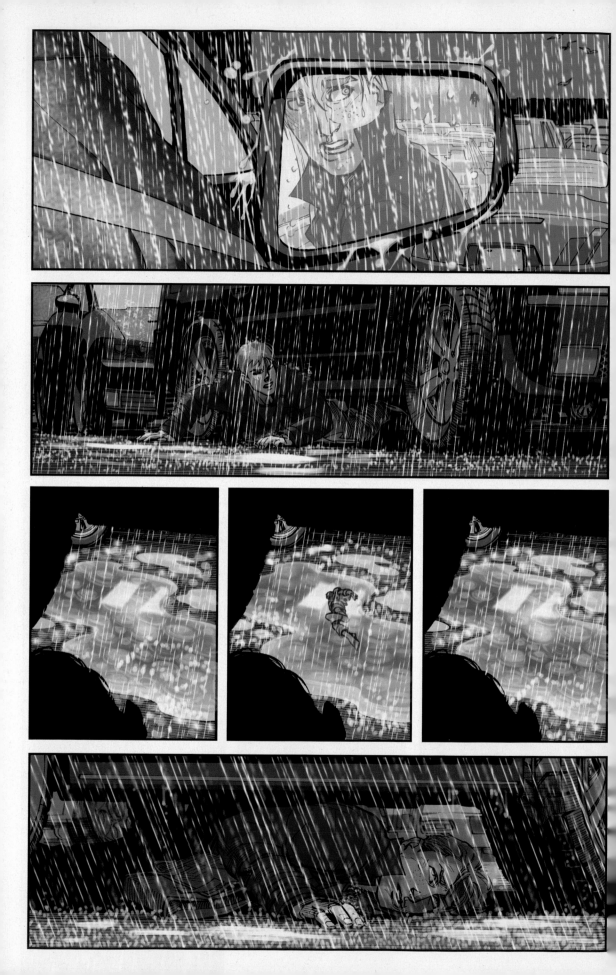

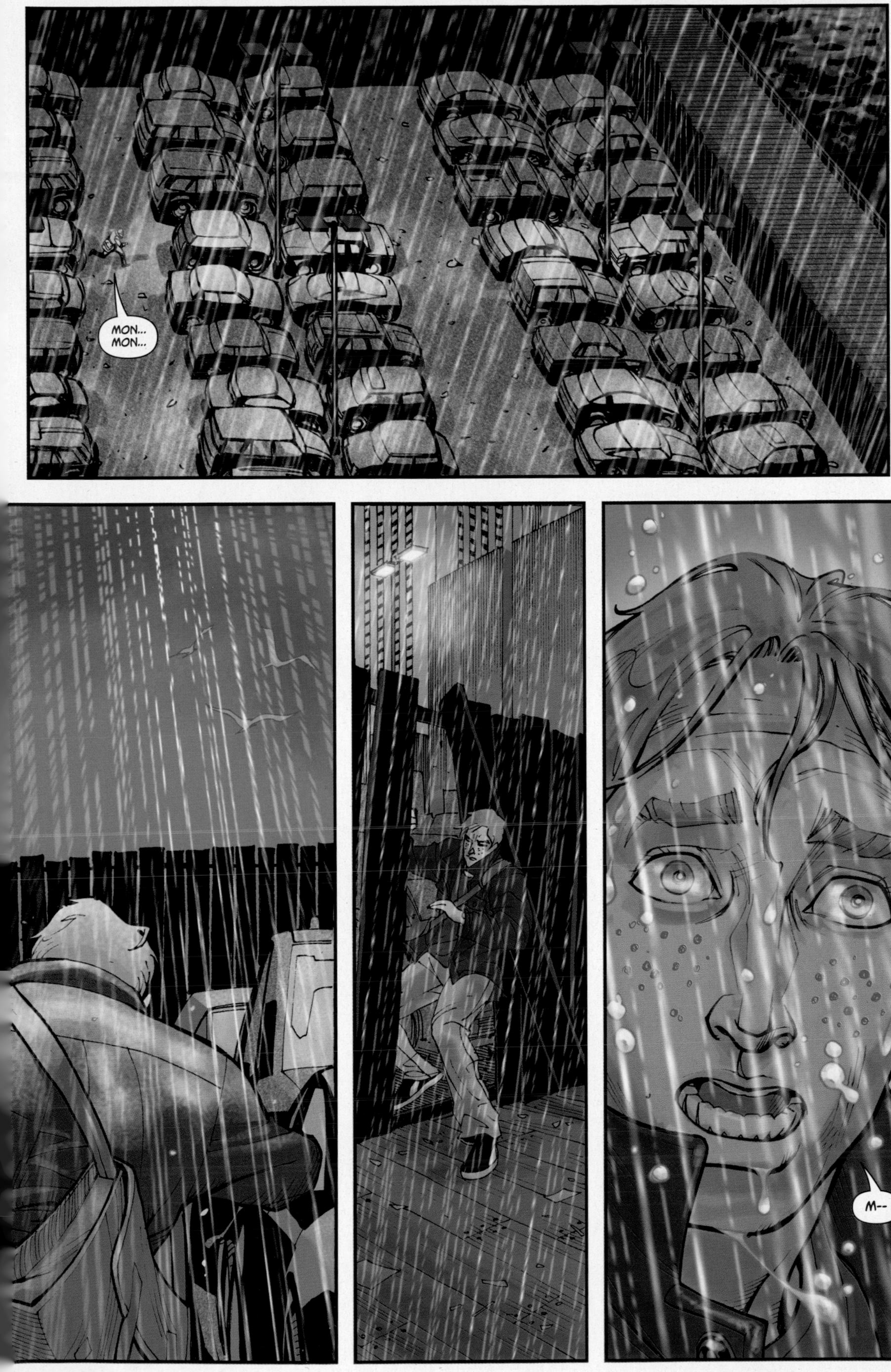
MON... MON...
M--

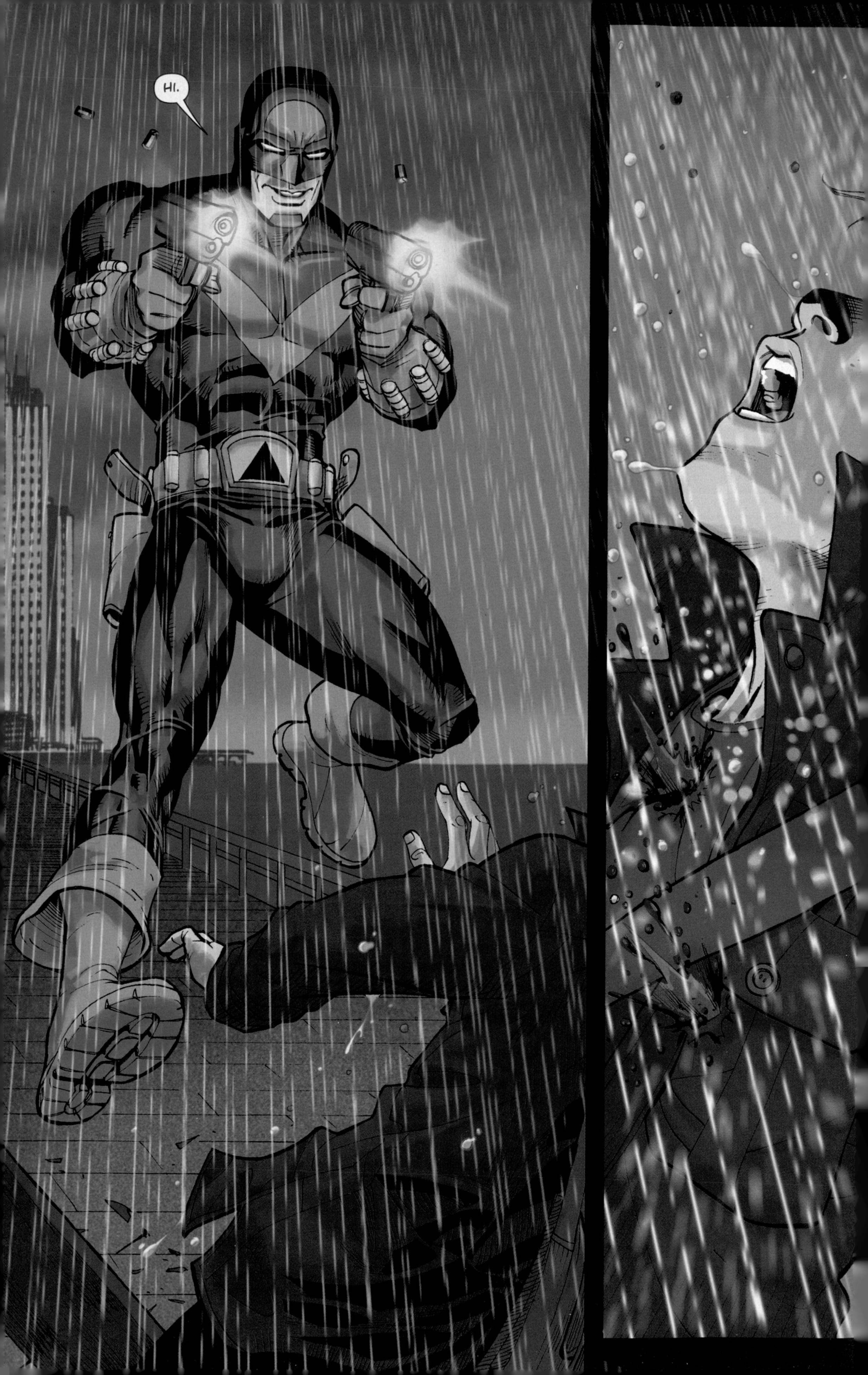
HI.

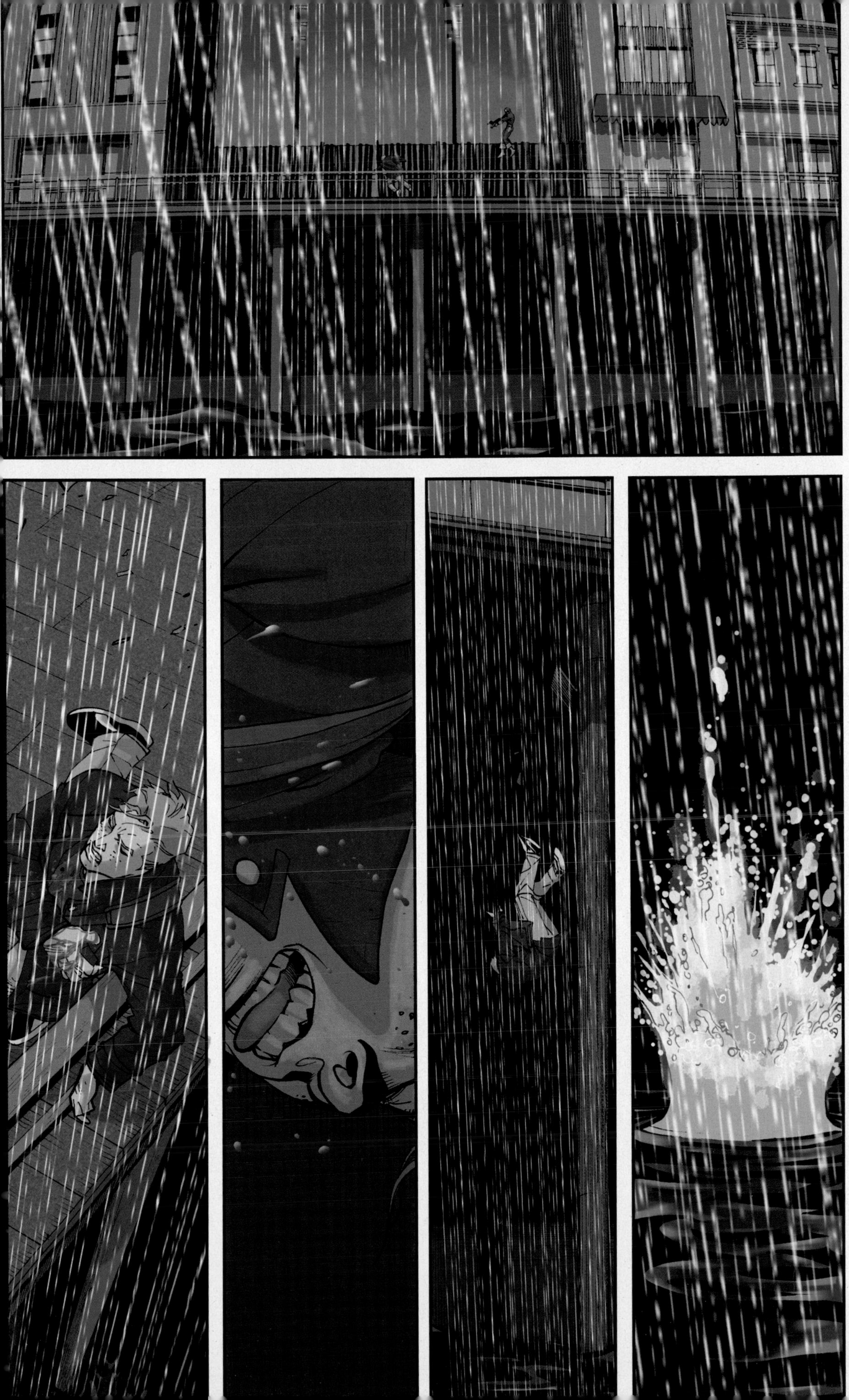

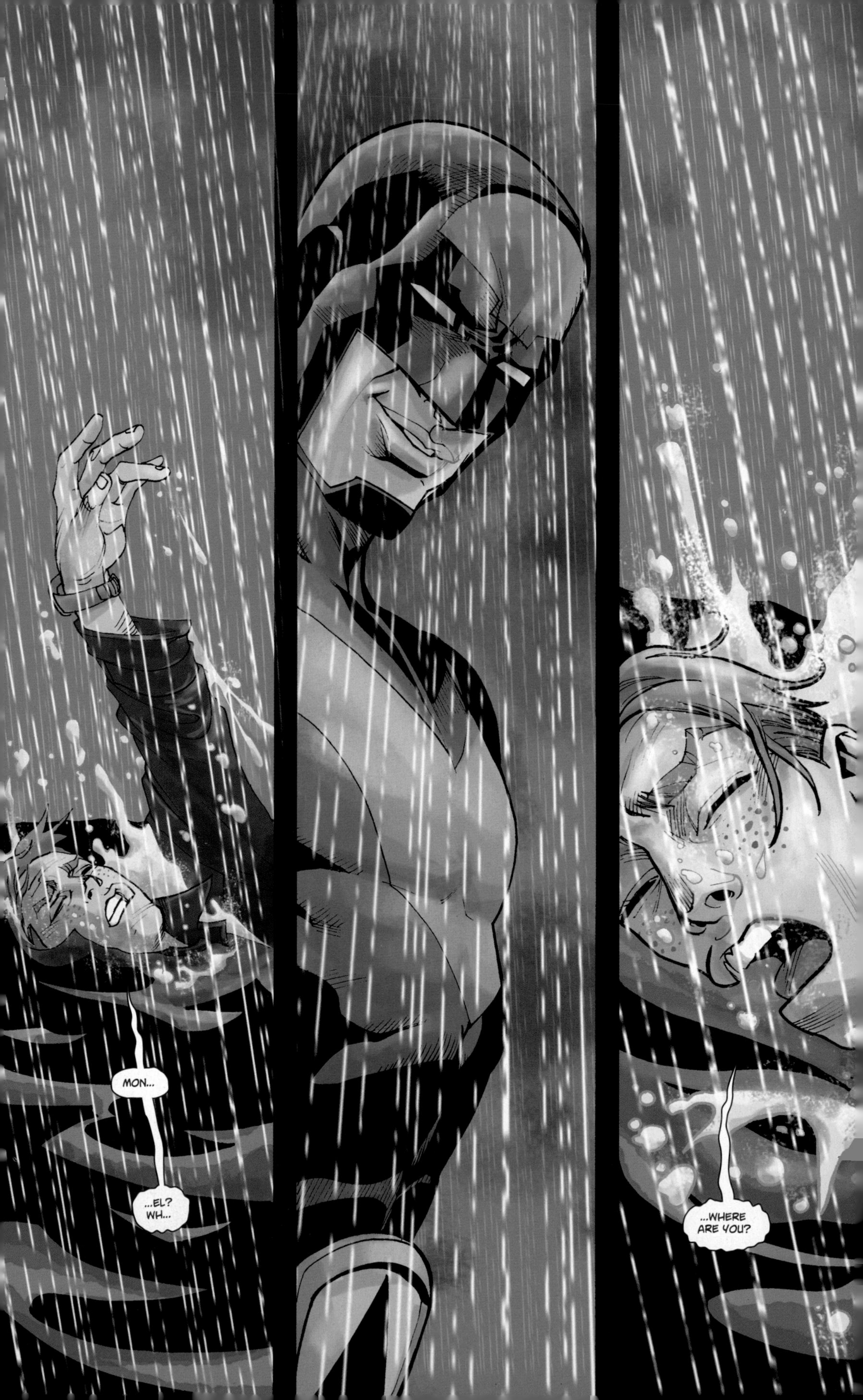
MON...
...EL? WH...
...WHERE ARE YOU?

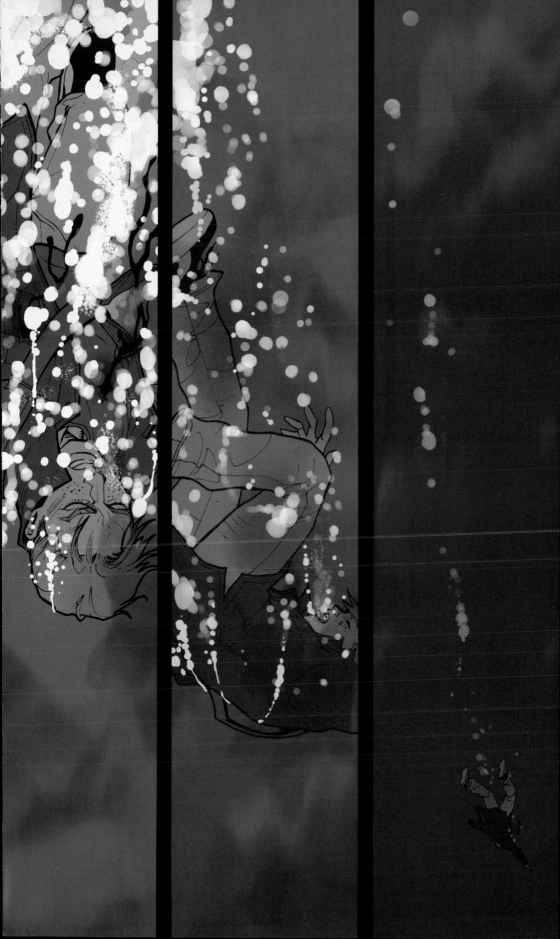

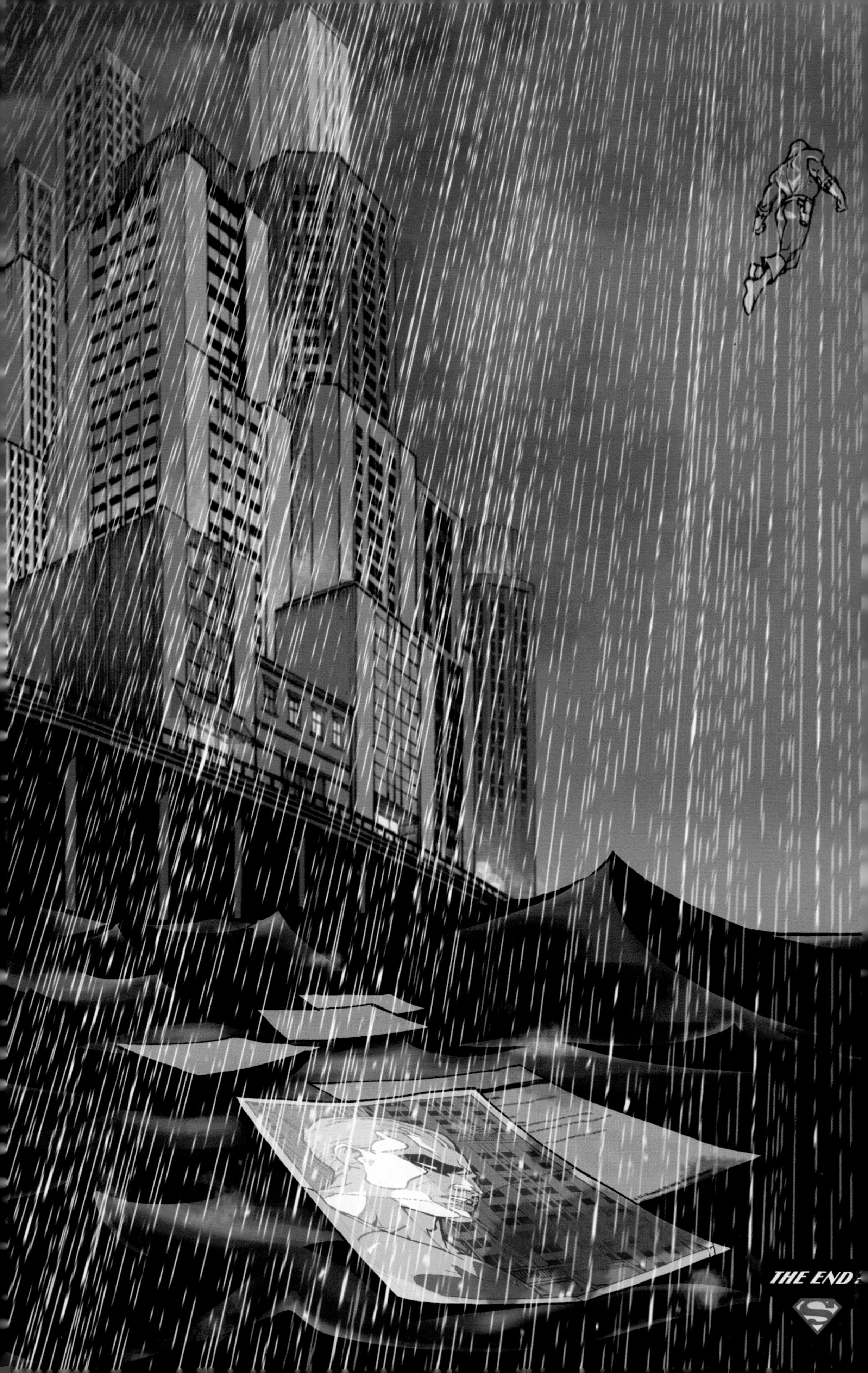
THE END?

<SUPERMAN: WORLD OF NEW KRYPTON 6 VARIANT>
BY **EDDY BARROWS** & **RUY JOSÉ** WITH **ROD REIS**

PROJECT 7734

BASE OF OPERATIONS: 7734 Bunker, location unknown

Created under the umbrella of safeguarding the planet against the threat of alien invasion, Project 7734 was created by General Sam Lane. Lane altered its focus to prepare the Earth to battle one thing: Kryptonians. More specifically, the Kryptonian called Superman.

The location of the bunker it operates from is unknown, but its cameras are seemingly everywhere, tracking everyone General Lane wants to keep his eyes on.

Text by JAMES ROBINSON, art by RENATO GUEDES & JOSÉ WILSON MAGALHÃES, color by DAVID CURIEL

GENERAL SAM LANE
BASE OF OPERATIONS: 7734 Headquarters and the world stage.

POWERS/ABILITIES: Lane is a genius-level strategist able to outplan and outthink almost anyone. As a combat-trained soldier, he remains a capable hand-to-hand combatant and a skilled marksman.

HISTORY: Hard-bitten, "take-no-prisoners" U.S. Army General Sam Lane died a hero's death defending Earth from the alien energy being known as Imperiex. His death, however, was faked, allowing Lane the freedom to set up black bag op Project 7734, based on his overriding distrust of aliens and Earth's need to prepare for any and all attacks from them.

Lane's focus, though, was **SUPERMAN**, whom he saw as a ticking bomb for America and the world. His distrust of the Man of Steel has grown to an intense level of hatred. The arrival of the citizens of Kandor on Earth and their relocation to New Krypton on the other side of Earth's sun has done nothing to curb that hatred.

Lane has secured an almost unlimited amount of funding that has allowed 7734 to acquire every form of weapon that it might need to combat the "Kryptonian Menace." These include metahumans, Kryptonite, magic and countless forms of high-tech weaponry. Lane has also managed to get both **SQUAD K** and the Human Defense Corps under his control, as well as ally himself with the mysterious **MIRABAI**.

Lane's strategy for the destruction of Superman and the Kryptonian race has slowly been unfolding. He has masterminded the death of Supergirl's father, Zor-El, as well as the infiltration within Kryptonian society of his daughter **LUCY** posing as Superwoman. And with the cooperation of **MORGAN EDGE**, he is building society's distrust of New Krypton. What his plans are for Mon-El, Nightwing and Flamebird have yet to be revealed, but based on his prior actions, it can be assumed they won't be good.

ATLAS
ALTER EGO: Tom Curtis
BASE OF OPERATIONS: 7734 Headquarters and wherever in the world General Lane wants someone hurt.

POWERS/ABILITIES: Atlas has superhuman strength, agility, and invulnerability sufficient to combat Superman.

HISTORY: A champion and **KING** in an ancient mythological era, mighty Atlas was snatched from the past by General Lane using Time Pool technology.

At first openly hostile to Lane, Atlas has made a wary truce with the general. He does Lane's bidding but has an agenda of his own that he has yet to reveal. On orders from Lane, Atlas attacked Superman as cover for 7734 to test its arsenal of magic on the Man of Steel. Superman ultimately defeated him with the help of Krypto. Since then, at the behest of Lane, he won the trust of **JOHN HENRY IRONS** only to betray the hero, for reasons still shrouded in mystery.

CODENAME: ASSASSIN
ALTER EGO: Jonathan Drew
BASE OF OPERATIONS: 7734 Headquarters and wherever in the world General Lane wants someone dead.

POWERS/ABILITIES: Drew has the power of telepathy, which allows him to sense emotions, read minds and project visions into the minds of others. He is telekinetic, allowing him to fly, generate force fields, and lift heavy objects with mental force alone. He is also a skilled marksman and superb hand-to-hand combatant.

HISTORY: Antioke University student **JONATHAN DREW** participated in an extrasensory perception experiment conducted by his professor, **DOCTOR ANDREW STONE**. During the experiment, Drew's mind was linked to a device that accidentally exploded. As a result he developed mental powers, which he used to punish the murderers of his sister.

Drew was recruited by the military for use in covert operations. For a brief time, he was head of security for Project Cadmus but was reassigned after he murdered the original Guardian. At some point he was recruited to General Lane's Project 7734 and now serves as Lane's staunchest ally and supporter. In the course of following Lane's orders, Drew has murdered Stone and the alien **DUBBILEX**, among others. He was unsuccessful in killing Jimmy Olsen but awaits the order from Lane so he can try again.

METALLO

ALTER EGO: John Corben

BASE OF OPERATIONS: Project 7734 Bunker (location unknown); Metropolis

POWERS/ABILITIES: Metallo possesses a super hard skeleton laced with metallo, the alloy from which he draws his codename. Within his chest is a piece of Green Kryptonite, giving him the ability to harm, and eventually kill, Kryptonians.

HISTORY: JOHN CORBEN was [REDACTED BY THE U.S. ARMY - REDACTED BY THE U.S. ARMY - REDACTED BY THE U.S. ARMY - REDACTED BY THE U.S. ARMY - REDACTED BY THE U.S. ARMY] a test subject for [REDACTED BY THE U.S. ARMY - REDACTED BY THE U.S. ARMY] Kryptonite heart and a metallic alloy lacing his chest cavity. Naming himself Metallo after the type of metal in his body, Corben [REDACTED BY THE U.S. ARMY - REDACTED BY THE U.S. ARMY] and a long history with Lois Lane.

Corben was stunned when the Green Kryptonite in his chest was able to take down the Man of Steel, but was eventually stopped by Superman. The once [REDACTED BY THE U.S. ARMY] was now a full-fledged supervillain.

Recently, Metallo has been recruited into Project: 7734 by **GENERAL LANE**. He and Reactron were part of an elite team that infiltrated Kandor after its enlargement. They murdered several Kryptonians, including the Kryptonian leader **ZOR-EL**, before being evacuated from the city by Superwoman. Now a man wanted by the Kryptonian government, Metallo is smart enough to lie low before showing his face again.

REACTRON

ALTER EGO: Major Benjamin Krull

BASE OF OPERATIONS: Project 7734 Bunker (location unknown); Metropolis

POWERS/ABILITIES: Reactron has a piece of Gold Kryptonite embedded in his chest, giving him the ability to neutralize a Kryptonian's powers for approximately fifteen seconds. He's also able to fire blasts of energy from his hands.

HISTORY: BENJAMIN KRULL was a loser who didn't know what to do with his life until he joined the U.S. Army. One night, while guarding an experimental [REDACTED BY THE U.S. ARMY], Krull was injured. Knowing he was going to die, Dr. [REDACTED BY THE U.S. ARMY], the man in charge of Project [REDACTED BY THE U.S. ARMY], decided Krull needed a new uniform, one that they hoped would prolong his life: the StarSuit.

Soon after his initial defeat at the hands of Supergirl, Krull was approached by General Lane with an offer to join Project 7734. Krull accepted, and he was fitted for a new suit — one with a piece of Gold Kryptonite in the middle.

Reactron was part of an elite team that infiltrated Kandor when it appeared on Earth, and was directly responsible for the death of the Kryptonian leader Zor-El. It is unknown what the ramifications will be once a Kryptonian finally gets hold of him. Fortunately for him, the piece of Gold Kryptonite in his chest will make it a fair fight.

Text by STERLING GATES, art by FERNANDO DAGNINGO & RAÚL FERNANDEZ, color by PETE PANTAZIS